The Power of Specificity in Psychotherapy

The Power of Specificity in Psychotherapy

When Therapy Works—And When It Doesn't

Howard A. Bacal, MD

with Lucyann Carlton, PsyD, JD

JASON ARONSON

Lanham • Boulder • New York • Toronto • Plymouth, UK

Published by Jason Aronson
An imprint of Rowman & Littlefield Publishers, Inc.
A wholly owned subsidiary of The Rowman & Littlefield Publishing Group, Inc.
4501 Forbes Boulevard, Suite 200, Lanham, Maryland 20706
http://www.rowmanlittlefield.com

Estover Road, Plymouth PL6 7PY, United Kingdom

British Library Cataloguing in Publication Information Available

Library of Congress Cataloging-in-Publication Data
Bacal, Howard A.
The power of specificity in psychotherapy : when therapy works and when it doesn't / Howard A. Bacal ; with Lucyann Carlton.
p. ; cm.
Includes bibliographical references and index.
ISBN 978-0-7657-0769-7 (cloth : alk. paper) — ISBN 978-0-7657-0771-0 (electronic)
1. Psychotherapy. 2. Psychoanalysis. I. Carlton, Lucyann, 1949– II. Title.
[DNLM: 1. Psychotherapy—methods. 2. Psychoanalytic Theory. WM 420]
RC480.5.B18 2011
616.89'14—dc22

2010037642

™ The paper used in this publication meets the minimum requirements of American National Standard for Information Sciences—Permanence of Paper for Printed Library Materials, ANSI/NISO Z39.48-1992.

Printed in the United States of America

For Wheeler

The most beautiful experience we can have is the mysterious. It is the fundamental emotion that stands at the cradle of true art and true science.

—Albert Einstein, *The World As I See It*

Theory as theory is all right. But the moment you apply it to life, especially to the subjective life, the theory becomes mechanistic, a substitute for life, a factor in the vicious unconscious.

—D. H. Lawrence, *The Posthumorous Papers*

Every patient is the same as every other, yet completely different.

—Michael Balint, personal communication

Contents

Preface

This book is a voyage into the depths of the mind as it interacts with the minds of others. I have been on the psychoanalytic journey with my patients and my supervisees for over half a century, and with my own therapists and supervisors for substantial chunks of that time. My clinical work continues to bring me great satisfaction. It has also, at times, been accompanied by frustration, disappointment, discouragement, and failure. I too know what it is like to be on the couch when therapy is not working.

During my quest for therapeutic possibility, I drew attention to what seemed to me to be obvious, though curiously unrecognized: that the multiplicity of ways in which people experience therapeutic effect is matched only by the specificity of that experience. I called the therapist's contribution to this experience, "optimal responsiveness." And then I realized that within this approach to psychotherapy there lurked a theory that was just as obvious, but which was just as unrecognized: that the power of psychotherapy is in the specificity of the unique process of its particular participants. This book articulates specificity theory and its effect on clinical practice and on the teaching and learning of psychotherapy.

Specificity theory is a contemporary psychoanalytic process theory that is consistent with cutting edge neurobiological findings about the human mind: that it is continuously formed and created through ongoing selective interactions with itself and its environment. Specificity theory calls upon the psychoanalytic psychotherapist to hold in mind what follows from this reality: that each interaction between persons is unique, unpredictable, and specific to them and that moment.

Specificity theory illuminates therapeutic effect as centrally a function of the capacities and limitations of the particular therapist and patient to understand and respond to each other at any moment in time and over the course of the treatment. Attention to the specificity of unfolding process between that patient and that therapist enhances possibilities for achieving maximal therapeutic effect, and clarifies why this may not be happening.

There are neither guidelines for technique nor textbooks for understanding a patient or the course of the work. Specificity theory is a different order of theory. Established psychoanalytic theories and their approaches are generalities that may or may not be effectively applied within the emerging process of any particular therapeutic dyad. The overarching focus of specificity theory is co-creative discovery of reciprocal responsiveness that will optimally meet the patient's therapeutic needs and that is possible for that therapist.

The last chapter of our book describes the usefulness of the perspectives of specificity theory in the training for psychotherapy—in particular, within supervision. Our sensitivity, as supervisors, to the specificity of process within both the treatment and the supervisory dyad as we engage with each student around her case material, can deepen understanding and the capacity to utilize it. As we learn—as both supervisors and supervisees—to apprehend the power of the specificity of process, we can become better teachers for our students as well as better therapists for our patients.

ACKNOWLEDGMENTS

While I take full responsibility for the content of this book, much of it reflects collaboration over several years with my colleague and friend, Lucyann Carlton. I am especially grateful to Dr. Carlton for her contributions to specificity theory from neurobiology and for her in-depth distinction between process and structure, contributions that have enriched and developed specificity theory much more than I ever could have done on my own.

Howard A. Bacal

1

The Need for a New Theory of Therapy

"Another theory of psychotherapy?!"[1] you might inquire, with perhaps a tone of impatience, or even exasperation. Do we really need to add more postulates to an already bewildering array of more or less established doctrine? And if so, why this one? Specificity theory—the response to these challenges—is not another traditional structured theory that proclaims the truth about human affliction and its cure. It is a process theory that promotes powerful new ways of understanding and engaging the practice of psychotherapy, and of apprehending why treatment is not proceeding optimally. Specificity theory also offers new perspectives on the training of psychoanalytic psychotherapists.

While traditional psychoanalytic theories have yielded manifold benefits, we need a theory of therapy that accounts not only for the organized, stable, predictable, and universal patterns of mental life, and for its unpredictable, nonlinear patterning; we need a theory that gives substance to the unique and specific development and functioning of the mind in process with other minds. We also need a theory that is consonant with current neurobiological understanding of mind which recognizes its uniqueness as a biological system—in particular, that the human mind is continuously formed and transformed through ongoing selective, specific interactions with itself and its environment. Closely related to this is the need for a theory of therapy that promotes the efforts of our brain to forestall closure prematurely. Edelman (2004) has demonstrated that when the brain is confronted with novel stimuli, the neuronal connections are actively at work to organize and make sense of the stimuli until a familiar pattern is forged or attained. The brain is not trying to form a scientifically accurate picture of the world, per se, but one that is familiar and meaningful to the perceiver.

With this innate biological pull toward closure, curiosity and attention to the novel and unique is blunted. Specificity theory helps us counter this inherent tendency—which can be reinforced by the application of structured theories—and to reengage our curiosity to search out other elements that may transcend the relevance of these theories for the patient.

SPECIFICITY THEORY—A FIRST DEFINITION

Specificity theory is a systems theory of psychotherapy. Its central tenet is that effective treatment is a function of the unique and specific unfolding process between its participants. Therapeutic possibility is ultimately determined by the specificity of the co-created process of any particular dyad.[2] It is determined by the capacities and limitations of each therapist and patient to understand and respond to each other. Specificity theory does not provide the practitioner with do's and don'ts. Rather, through its in-depth focus on process, it illuminates how a therapist may practice as best she can with each particular patient. When a therapist fully comprehends the reach and power of specificity of human relatedness at every level and at every moment in time, the application of both explicitly formulated theory, and implicit "theory," within the clinical situation becomes more apparent, and is enhanced.

THE CONCEPT OF "PROCESS"

We use the term, "process," in a way that differs from its every day understanding; for example, to describe the entire therapeutic enterprise, as in "the psychoanalytic process is complex"; or to describe a particular facet of treatment, as in "the process of joining the patient" or the "process of making the unconscious conscious." In the instance of theory comparison, we use the term "process" to denote a fundamental defining quality of a particular kind of theoretical construct. "Process" theory refers to the defining essence of therapy and of mental life of the person as comprised of sustained, ongoing phenomena emerging from and alterable by the interactions between the therapist and patient. In contrast, "structure" theories view the mind, development, cure, and technique as definite, objectively knowable universal and predictable entities. We address this distinction more fully in chapter 2 where we consider the use of theory in psychotherapeutic practice. Our use of the word, "process," also refers to a theory of mind, which we describe in chapter 4, that regards development, illness, therapeutic action and cure as sustained phenomena without a predetermined universal end state. From these perspectives, stable organizations are achieved over time, but are always subject to change, unpredictably, as a result of ongoing relations.

HOW WE STUDY THERAPEUTIC EFFECT

Therapeutic effect or whether change has occurred can be considered in two major domains: therapeutic *outcome*, and therapeutic *process*, which may or may not be related. Assessment of therapeutic outcome, by whatever criteria and whatever methodology, is the province of formal psychotherapy research.[3] Consideration of therapeutic process—which is about how therapy happens, or does not—requires that we study it from a different point of view, in effect, through the lens of the specificity of process.

I actually encountered a non-linear theory of therapeutic specificity for the first time during my participation in a formal psychotherapy research project. None of us who were involved in the research recognized this to be so at the time. Yet, such theory was, in effect, embedded within the project's unique methodology to assess outcome, and it basically determined how we evaluated our results. The project, which was conducted under the leadership of D. H. Malan at the Tavistock Clinic in London in the 1960s, entailed the assessment of the psychological status of a series of formally untreated "neurotic" patients who had been seen at intake at the Clinic at least two years previously (see Malan, Bacal, Heath, & Balfour, 1968). The criterion for a person's inclusion in the study was never having seen a psychologist or a psychiatrist more than twice in his or her life. Our aim was to explore at follow up interview the extent to which improvement had occurred over time in particular ways without formal treatment.[4]

After reading the initial intake for each patient, each of us independently offered his view of what would constitute progress specific for that patient if he were to have undertaken a course of psychotherapy. In other words, we considered the attainment of true change neither on the basis of relief of symptoms nor on the basis of the usual general categories of healthy social and psychological functioning, but rather upon significant amelioration in specific aspects of the patient's life situation that appeared to reflect change in his or her susceptibility to experiences that stressed particular vulnerabilities.

While we rarely agreed when it came to formulating the patient's dynamics on the basis of traditional psychoanalytic concepts (even though our theoretical differences were minimal), we had little trouble reaching a consensus on what would constitute improvement for the particular patient. Further outcome research on our study itself (Malan, Heath, Bacal, & Balfour, 1975) also indicated the operation of an unpredictable process of specificity. It turned out that those who were most significantly changed on psychodynamic criteria had either experienced significant therapeutic effect from particular experience in their initial consultation, or/and were subsequently able to "use" similar, specific "therapeutic" responsiveness from others.

While this psychodynamic research illuminated the specificity of outcome for the particular individual, it also suggested that therapeutic process that led to whatever outcome is less dependent upon application of any particular formal theory and more a function of the specificity of dyadic interaction. In effect, the research findings implied that a different kind of theory would be needed in order to learn more about this—a theory that focuses upon and conceptualizes the very nature of a therapeutic process.

When the therapeutic method is structured in a linear mode, such as psychopharmacological therapies, cognitive behavioral therapy, or other therapies guided by structured theories, process and outcome will be evidently related. We can follow how the intervention leads to the result. Symptom identification and therapeutic intervention are linked in a predictable way with evidence-based outcome studies. They may not be so clearly related, though, if the therapeutic method is less structured. Unless psychotherapy is structured and confined to certain issues, as in brief therapy or cognitive behavior therapy, the problems patients initially proffer may not only "change" as therapy deepens, but the process whereby change occurs may itself become impacted by unpredictable factors. Here, we enter the world of non-linear systems,[5] where we are challenged to discern what or who has been responsible for therapeutic effect (Coburn, 2002; Galatzer-Levy, 2007).[6] Psychoanalytic treatment, in many of its forms, comes under this rubric. In this situation, we require a theory of therapeutic effect that is not only consistent with the domain that it considers—that is, a process theory—but also one that directs our focus to its ineluctable specificity.

SPECIFICITY THEORY AND OTHER PROCESS THEORIES

The perspectives of specificity theory are consistent with aspects of other process theories, such as intersubjective systems theory and complexity theory. These include intersubjective systems theory's view that "psychological phenomena [both developmentally and in the psychoanalytic situation] take form within an intersubjective field constituted by the interacting subjective worlds of child and caregiver or of patient and analyst" (Stolorow, in Skelton, ed., 2006, p. 250). The perspectives of specificity theory also concur with Stolorow's extension of his intersubjective perspective into contextualism as "a broad-based philosophy of psychoanalytic practice" (Stolorow, in Skelton, ed., 2006, p. 250), a philosophy wherein "standards of knowledge and justification vary with context" (see Brower, 2000, p. 174).

Complexity theory has been described by many authors from both without and within the world of psychotherapy, beginning with the classic article of Thelen and Smith (1994), and Thelen, E. (2005). In effect, specificity theory takes up the challenge proffered by Coburn (2002) to apply the experience-distant, hypothetical constructs of complexity theory to the clinical situation. This subject has also been addressed by Weisel-Barth (2006) (see also Richetta [2010], for a comparison of the application of complexity theory and specificity theory in a particular clinical case).

In addition to contextuality, points of contact between specificity theory and complexity theory comprise non-linearity—the quality of a function that expresses a relationship that is not one of predictable relations, that is, small perturbations may yield large effects and vice-versa; and complexity itself, that is, that any behavior, whether mental or physical, results from many heterogeneous constituent parts that interact to produce a coherent pattern (Thelen, 2005), a pattern that is organized and coherent, but nevertheless continually altered through ongoing relations among the constituents. As Coburn (2002) states, experience takes shape and continues to transform dynamically out of multiple, interpenetrating systems. While systems may seem at times to recede into the background within the context of an analytic situation, they "never die, and . . . we continue to be 'of' all of them" (p. 666). Further, both complexity theory and specificity theory regard mental life in systems terms, that is, both theories understand minds to be continuously and dynamically formed, self organizing, and continuous in time. In other words, such systems organize patterns from multiple constituent parts continuously in time, and dynamically, which, "in the language of complexity theory means that the state of the system at any time depends on its previous states and is the starting point for future states" (Thelen, p. 261). They also exhibit dynamic stability, that is, systems that organize into patterns may have different degrees of stability and flexibility (ibid., p. 261).

While specificity theory shares these field properties with other systems theories, its focus differs. Specificity theory is centrally concerned with therapeutic possibility. On the one hand, structure theories assert, a priori, that certain kinds of interventions based upon them will determine therapeutic effect. A radical systems sensibility would maintain that what accounts for therapeutic effect within ongoing process is indeterminable. Specificity theory moves the therapist to explore, within the uniquely unfolding process of the therapeutic dyad, how her responsiveness may make a therapeutic difference.

Specificity theory also offers a valuable new dimension to the education of the psychoanalytic psychotherapist, a topic we consider in depth in our final chapter. Focusing on the specificity of process within supervisory situations—both individually and in groups—educates the student not only about how to become the clinician he or she can be with that particular patient, but also how she or he may become a better therapist for all of them.

NOTES

1. Unless other wise indicated, the terms "psychotherapy" and "psychoanalytic therapy" are used in this book synonymously to designate a relatively non-linear psychotherapeutic process.
2. While our focus is the dyad, this applies to any therapeutic constellation, such as a therapy group or a family in family therapy.
3. See *The Edinburgh International Encyclopaedia of Psychoanalysis*, "Outcome" entry, 2006, 343–346, for a succinct history of outcome research in psychoanalysis.
4. Our intent was to establish a baseline in order to challenge H. J. Eyesenck's (1952) hypothesis that, in psychotherapy, one-third of patients will improve, one-third will get worse, and one-third will remain the same. On the basis of our study of "untreated" patients, Eyesenck turned out to be right, on symptomatic criteria, but not on psychodynamic criteria (see Malan, Bacal, Heath, & Balfour, 1968).
5. In this book, "system" and "process" may seem to be used interchangeably, but their meanings are not identical. A system refers to a group of constituent parts that stand in relationship one to the other, i.e., a change in one affects a change in the other. Process, within this work, refers to a focus on the relationship that pertains in a system. In other words, in a process theory, the attention is more on the relatedness and movement among the constituent parts of the system, than on the constituent parts themselves. A process theory recognizes the continual changeability of the parts, parts that may appear to be self-contained structures, but in fact are not.
6. See also Galatzer-Levy (2002), where he introduces mathematical understanding of "emergence" to posit that each analytic dyad is unique with unique and unpredictable exchanges and outcomes.

2

The Use of Theory in Psychoanalytic Practice

THE LIMITATIONS OF STRUCTURE THEORY

Our use of theory of one sort or another in psychoanalytic practice is indispensable and inevitable, yet its usage poses discernible problems that are not infrequently shoved under the couch. Theory can be a helpful partner in our work; but it can also lead us astray, or get in our way. Although we do not openly acknowledge it, we tend to look to our preferred theories, consciously or unconsciously, to inform our understanding and to advise our responses to our patients. These theories are the ones that we have come to feel comfortable working with, the ones that we come to regard as truth. And if we have been trained as psychoanalysts, they will tend to reflect the beliefs of the analytic institutes where we have been trained, or the analytic societies or groups with which we are affiliated.

When Freud first led us from the chaos of psychological ignorance into the order of psychoanalytic theory, he understood emotional suffering, and even certain physical impairments as arising from mental determinants. Over his lifetime Freud developed a nomothetic theory of human development, and of psychological illness, health, and cure. That is, Freud's theories involved the formulation of general or universal laws that were premised upon an ordered and structured view of mental life, upon which definitive techniques of psychoanalytic treatment were based. Many analysts have continued to follow Freud's dicta. Freud's critics—a number of them ultimately hailed as psychoanalytic pioneers—have since elaborated many other theories and different ways of applying them. While these theories differ in their conceptualizations and modes of practice, each is premised on assumptions of order, continuity, and universality in human development. It is an open secret—yet one also largely unacknowledged—that our formally articulated theories simply do not always—and sometimes never—account for what happens in treatment, either when it is successful or when it fails, from either the patient's or the therapist's vantage point. Yet, we continue to use these theories as the basis for both apprehending *the* psychological truths about our patients and as guides for our interventions.

RESPONSES TO THE CONSTRAINTS OF FORMAL THEORY

Some recent contemporary responses to the constraints of formal theory have been to embrace the value of spontaneity and improvisation (Ringstrom, 2001, 2010; Kindler, 2010) or to place special value upon something other than interpretation (Stern et al., 1998, but see Nahum, 2005). As valuable as this may be in certain instances, we cannot avoid using "theories" or "models" of one sort or another; they comprise a significant part of who we are and will inevitably influence our responses to our patients. So, how is the clinician to "choose" wisely?

Another response to multiple formal theories of psychotherapy has been an "eclectic" or pluralistic approach, that is, to utilize a model, or theory—or combinations of these—with regard to their apparent applicability to a particular patient's problems (see Connors, 2010). And yet a third approach has been an "integrative" approach, that is, to view all theories as "true" but simply reflecting differing dimensions of human experience or reflecting differing points on a continuum of human experience. At first glance, this would seem to be a reasonable way to proceed, either the eclectic or integrative approaches. Our response to Connors's paper, whose theme is the utility of cognitive behavioral therapy within psychodynamic psychotherapy is titled, "Who Can Do What, Therapeutically, With Whom, in What Way?" (Bacal & Carlton, 2010a). Trying to match model to patient from amongst the plethora of possibilities is not a simple, straightforward task. Consider the remarkable multiplicity of perspectives and approaches that reside within the rubric of psychotherapy, each of them privileging different aspects of the person in defining illness, treatment, and cure. A psychotherapist practicing in this twenty-first century is confronted with a daunting array of major schools of psychotherapy within which multiple theories abound, each with its own view of therapeutic action that is mediated through its corresponding prescribed—and proscribed—responses. Within the world of psychodynamic therapies, the schools of psychotherapy and psychoanalysis also vary in their focus on the past or present of the patient, the intrapsychic world of wishes, dreams and fantasies of the patient, or the interpersonal world of today's relationships with others inside or outside of the consulting room. Integrationists and eclectics attempt to honor the claim of each model for ubiquitous therapeutic relevance by trying to find commonalities amongst them and diverse application for them. Yet here, too, we run into difficulty if we proceed on the assumption that it is possible to achieve theoretic "reliability" (note, for example, the difficulty we had in doing this during our outcome research at the Tavistock Clinic, in which our theoretical differences were minimal—see chapter 1).

Findings in contemporary ancillary fields of infant research (Sander, 2002; Lyons-Ruth, 2000, 2006; Stern et al., 1998; Beebe & Lachmann, 2002), neurobiology (Edelman, 1987, 1988, 1989), physics (Cilliers, 1998), mathematics (Prigogine, 1996), and epistemological philosophy (Gadamer, 1975) turn our attention to an equally compelling aspect of all biological life—the unorganized, discontinuous, unpredictable, and unique in the development and functioning of the human mind (see also Spruiell, 1993; Trop, Burke, & Trop, 2002). Contemporary theories in each of these disciplines recognize stable organizations and patterns, but give equal weight to their possible instability over time, and to their openness to change in sudden, unpredictable ways. These systems, or process, theories recognize that substantial change may result from seemingly small perturbations, and that stability may be maintained even in the face of massive stressors in the direction of change. Many traditional structure theories include elements of process, yet such hybrids or compromises are also premised upon assumptions of order, continuity, predictability, and universality in human development. If we do continue to recognize the usefulness of employing the concepts of multiple structure theories, what is the optimal way of utilizing them?

It occurred to me, at first somewhat whimsically, that any alternative way of proceeding would somehow have to include the tenets of established postulates, meet the requirements of those who place value on integration or eclecticism, and perhaps in some way even intrigue those empiricists who would incline toward turning their back on theory-making altogether. A dubiously possible achievement. But what if we think about this in a different way? *The application of a process theory of specificity does not require the integration of variegated theory, or model for eclecticism. The concepts that comprise the diverse theoretical perspectives of psychotherapy and psychoanalysis will continue to be variously useful, but as aspects of specific emerging process: Prescriptive application of structure theory yields to its specifically emerging relevance within the process of a particular therapeutic dyad (or other therapeutic constellation).*

A theory of this kind is playfully depicted in the parody about a local rabbi whose response was petitioned by two peasants to settle a dispute between them. The first man approached the rabbi with the complaint that his neighbor was repeatedly coming into his yard to milk his goat, which not only disturbed him, but also affected the goat, altering the nature of its milk. The rabbi listened carefully to the peasant and told him, "My good man, I understand; you are quite right." A short while later, the neighbor came in and explained at length to the rabbi why the goat was truly his, and that he was simply exercising his claim to it. The rabbi listened very carefully and then told him, "My good man, I understand; you are quite right in your claim." After the man left, the rabbi's assistant, who had been listening to both claimants and to the rabbi's responses to each of them, turned to the rabbi in total amazement and asked, "How can you think both of them to be right?!" To which the rabbi replied, "You know, you're right, too."

While this situation overtly deals with disputation around ownership and who gets whose goat—and one might be tempted to mine it for caricatures that reflect our various therapeutic approaches and formal theories, and our relationships with each other about them—we offer it not only as a transparently exaggerated apologue to poke fun at attempts to reconcile diversity. We also offer it to seriously suggest that one can have a theory that could honor the validity of even widely divergent perspectives, within process—a theory that therapists as well as rabbis could use wisely. If we look more closely at this little story, we can discern that the rabbi was conveying that he not only apprehended the subjectivity of each of the protagonists—as well as that of his assistant—he conveyed that he felt that each of their theories about the situation could be right.

The apparent silliness of our rabbi's responses can be taken as a metaphoric invitation to consider that a theory that places process and uniqueness at the center of our attention may in fact allow us both to utilize the tenets of established postulates, meet the requirements of those who place value on integration or eclecticism, and possibly even interest those who are skeptical of theory-making altogether. Such a theory would take a perspective on the therapeutic endeavor that is different from a structure paradigm whose tenets determine truth, a priori, and concomitantly prescribe responses. A theory that accords uniqueness priority could enhance the possibilities for therapeutic effect. While retaining the potential utility of the multiplicity of formal perspectives, our theory would preeminently approach the particularity of each clinical situation without peremptory prescription or proscription.[1] Specificity theory gives substance to the view that every theory of psychotherapy and its methodology is potentially as "right" as it is "wrong"; but that its usefulness depends upon its relevance to the uniqueness of the process in which the particular individuals are participating.

While we think of a structure theory, in contrast to specificity theory, as prescribing a particular response, we need to recognize that any particular orientation, including specificity theory, will influence the dyad in a particular way. Once a theory formulates its view of therapeutic action, the analyst will be attuned to "this" and less "that." With specificity theory, we attempt to discern what is the anticipated or desired or needed response; yet specificity theory is unique in then saying that we continue to examine whether the response was helpful and to alter our responsiveness as best we can. Specific responses that are deemed therapeutic are always in process, and the "process of treatment" is thereby affected in a particular way that will yield a different tilt in the therapy than one that has a more singular notion of therapeutic action.

In other words, if structure theories are understood within the overarching perspective of the specificity of process, a syncretic use of theory emerges. Structure theories are not discarded by specificity theory. Structure theories are useful in at least two ways: they provide a particular structure to consider, and they may serve as a probe to expand our observational field. At the same time, they may occlude aspects of the observational field and impose a structure that is not applicable specifically to a particular patient/therapist pair.

In disputing the psychoanalytic dictum that therapeutic effect is consequent upon only one mode of therapeutic action—verbal explication—I conceptualized a way of working that I called "optimal responsiveness," which also implied that in any specific instance or context, responses based upon any of our formal theories may or may not be therapeutically applicable to a particular patient (Bacal, 1985, 1998). As the therapist works in this way with her patient, the treatment is affected in a particular way that will yield a different tilt to it. More concepts, theories, and models can thereby be utilized more relevantly, in contrast to the presumptive application of a more singular notion of effective therapeutic action. The concept, optimal responsiveness, in effect questioned the validity of a universality of mind-set that is intrinsic to all traditional psychoanalytic theory. In other words, it implied an underlying theory of therapeutic specificity.

In contrast to prescribed therapeutic methodology arising from the application of a structure theory, whose tenets direct the therapist to apply prescribed responses in order to achieve therapeutic effect, therapeutic possibility informed by specificity theory emerges within process as the capacity of that dyad to actualize what could be specifically therapeutic for that patient. Therapeutic action, thus informed, will inevitably be imbued with one or another "theory" or "model," but it will come into play in a different way.

FROM THE UNIVERSALITY OF STRUCTURE TO THE SPECIFICITY OF PROCESS: A DIFFERENT ORDER OF THEORY

Concurrent with her elaboration of the neurobiological underpinnings of specificity theory (see chapter 4), Lucyann Carlton drew attention to a quality of process that is inherent in specificity theory in contrast to a quality of structure that characterizes traditional psychoanalytic theories (Carlton, personal communication, 2004; Carlton, 2009). She pointed out that all theories of psychotherapy are premised upon a theory of mind, its development, health, illness, and cure, and that while the various schools of psychotherapy offer numerous and contrasting views of mind, a fundamental distinction among theories can be drawn from their definitional essence of the nature of the mind either as structure or as process, or system.[2] Carlton has described how defining the nature of the mind as structure or process has important implications for how our theories affect our practice. When the mind is understood as structure, it is objectively knowable and develops and functions in predictable ways primarily according to inherent design. The metaphorical use of the word "structure" (whether as a steam engine, computer, or multi-story building) to define the mind invokes similarities to building or fixing an object with a blueprint for the desired product, and with agreed-upon techniques for its successful completion. Within the world of psychoanalysis, the mind, from this perspective, is conceived of as a type of object with a discernible inside and outside and with a defined organization that is separate from the analyst: for example, Freud's structural model of a mind comprising an id, ego, and super-ego that is formed as the child passes through specified stages of psycho-sexual development and motivated by the force of two innate drives. Its study assumes that the analyst can learn about the mind of another through cause-and-effect, linear reasoning. Structure theories are the type of theory with which we are most familiar as psychoanalysts and psychotherapists, such as classical psychoanalytic theory, ego-psychology, object relations, Kleinian, Lacanian theory, or self psychology. This type of theory offers universally applicable concepts for understanding the patient, and prescriptive and proscriptive guidelines for responding therapeutically. In contrast, a theory of therapy that privileges process defines the mind as process that is always in process, and that interaction between minds is unique, unpredictable, and non-replicable. This view of mind derives from the neurobiologic research of Gerald Edelman about the anatomy and function of the brain, which we will consider in chapter 4.

From the perspective of specificity theory, there are neither guidelines for technique nor textbooks for understanding a patient. Established psychoanalytic theories, their structured concepts, and the therapeutic approaches they prescribe are generalities that may or may not illuminate the particularity of process for each dyad.

Carlton's conceptualization of process significantly advances our understanding of specificity theory as a different order of theory—a theory that operates at a level of abstraction that leads us to consider that whatever "specificities" emerge, they are all specific to who the participants are in their particular process. Thus, we may talk of a myriad of qualities that contribute to the specificity of fit, or of linkage, in variegated ways: origin, culture, outlook, humor, values, development, therapeutic quest, motivation etc. In other words, we are speaking about a process, or systems, theory, in which specificity is its central attribute (Carlton 2009).

NOTES

1. Lewis (2009) has questioned whether "the present focus on the particularity of each patient/analyst dyad might be just as extreme, in its own way, as any psychoanalytic theory that seeks to universalize human psychodynamics. . . It is my hope that human sameness and the uniqueness of our own subjectivities can exist side by side." Our overall response to this challenge is, in effect, offered at various points within this book, where we address its spuriousness as a polemic. In particular, the answer to Lewis's question is twofold: the higher order theory, with regard to therapeutic possibility, is that of the particularity of process of the dyad, which does not preclude application, at a lower level, of structure theory as it may relevantly emerge in process. Second, the recognition of the uniqueness of the individual and of dyadic process requires the application of a universal human capacity (and perhaps that of some animals) for empathy (see Schwaber, 2010, p. 166)—which itself is variable and dyadically specific—not the invocation of a theory that is regarded as universally relevant.

2. See note 5, chapter 1.

3

How Specificity Theory Changes Clinical Practice

Specificity theory, in accord with other process theories, recognizes that we cannot know a priori how any particular response or dyadic interaction will affect either the patient, the analyst, or their relationship, but what we do know is that what constitutes therapeutic action, too, is specific; that is, what may be therapeutic, and what can be therapeutic, for any particular patient is determined by the specific capacities of that particular dyad (or other therapeutic constellation) and the specificity of their unfolding process. With specificity theory the clinician's focus is directed less to specific techniques and more to the specificity of the person and the process itself.

Specificity theory significantly influences how we use psychoanalytic theories that do posit universal motives, stages of development, and curative interventions. Specificity theory as a *process* theory shifts our focus from a *designated response* as the sine qua non of psychoanalytic cure to a *process* that seeks to *discover* within each dyad that which might be healing. However, not only is it advisable that we not "know" in advance who the patient is, as Bion recommends (see Bion, 1967), we do not know how we may optimally be with him therapeutically from moment to moment, until we discover this through the unfolding specificity of our process.

Formal, and informal, structure theories are variously necessary and all may emerge within process. No psychoanalytic theory that purports ubiquitous application can apply to psychoanalysis when viewed *as process*. Freud analyzed the free associations of the analysand to discover the repressed in the unconscious, on the basis of his theory of "mind." Analysts since Freud have attended to a variety of data—perhaps mainly to their empathic perceptions—which they "analyze," and respond to in various ways on the basis of various structured theories, in order to offer their patients optimal therapeutic experience. Specificity theory not only recognizes the variegated ways in which patients may experience their therapists as responding optimally, it also avers that any organized understanding (structure theory, culture, technique, gender) *optimally emerges in process* as it may apply to apprehending and responding to the particular patient. Evelyne Schwaber's way of empathic listening to both her patient and herself implies this recognition of the therapeutic importance of specificity in emerging dyadic process (Schwaber, 1981, 2010).

Both Lewis Aron and Jessica Benjamin convey their recognition of specificity as central to both theory and practice. Benjamin quotes Mitchell (1997) "[who contends that] transformation occurs when the analyst *stops trying* to live up to a generic, uncontaminated solution, and finds instead the custom-fitted solution for a particular patient" (Benjamin, 2004, p. 41). Benjamin concludes her article with the observation that "[a]ll patients, in individual ways, place their hopes for the therapeutic process in us, and for each one, we must use our own subjectivity in a different way to struggle through to a specific solution" (p. 18). Aron concludes his colloquium contribution on November 14, 2006, by commenting, "What is wonderful about contemporary psychoanalysis . . . is that we do not all have to work the same way or expect that we will each negotiate each therapeutic moment the same way—following one book or rather narrow technical prescriptions. This is neither eclectic nor a matter of throwing away the book—it is about having a new kind of book that allows for individualized, negotiated, more personal, and also less predictable responsiveness."

Specificity theory in effect conceptualizes Benjamin's and Aron's views about how therapy happens, at a higher order of abstraction than theories of structure. Specificity theory understands psychoanalytic treatment as optimally constituting a process of co-creative discovery in every instance as to what "theory" may emerge as relevant and useful. This contrasts sharply with the traditional utilization of structure theories that, in effect, inform us, a priori, how we should be therapeutically with our patients. While structure theories guide our interventions, specificity theory allows us to creatively co-discover, through the particularity of each unfolding relationship, how we may, or may not, be therapeutic with a particular patient at any moment in time. At the same time, we also discover, through our process, consciously or unconsciously, what concepts, models, or perspectives may usefully inform how each of us may be therapeutic with a particular patient at any moment in time. So that rather than *reaching* for the tenets of any formal theory or model in order to understand or respond to a particular patient, we position ourselves receptively so that we may allow for their application as they may—or may not—emerge[1] as potentially relevant in understanding and responding therapeutically to that patient. In focusing on therapeutic effect at the level of the *specificity of process*, we develop *a theory of therapeutic specificity*, which enables a very different, yet potentially more enlightened and effective utilization of both formally established concepts, and a host of other "informal" theory that every analyst as well as every analysand, ineluctably brings to the therapeutic endeavor.

CLINICAL ILLUSTRATIONS

Here are two clinical examples, offered by Lucyann Carlton, which illustrate how specificity theory changes our practice. The examples comprise vignettes from two different analyses, one in which the author was the analysand and one in which she was the analyst. The first analysis was guided by classical psychoanalytic theory and the second by specificity theory. The vignettes draw attention to the essential theoretic difference between the two types of theory—structure theory, associated with "known" response, and process theory, which determines a position of not-knowing. They also illustrate the clinical difference as we note the shift from responding on the basis of established tenets to awareness of the potential for the therapy when the analyst considers the significance of how she can be within the specific context of treatment with the particular patient.

Practice That Privileges a Traditional Structure Theory

When I first met with my analyst, we sat face to face as she assessed my analyzability. I told her of my current difficulties, family history, and personal development. She shared with me that she had her doubts about me. I seemed to be someone who liked to be the "captain of her own ship." "This does not bode well for analysis," my analyst opined. However, she suggested a trial few months. She set forth the rules of engagement. "Each time you come in, you will lie down on the couch. You will begin talking, saying anything that comes to your mind. I will be quiet. I will listen, and only say something when I have something to say." And so our odyssey began.

I did not understand how the assumption of control over my own life would render me unfit for treatment. How did anyone navigate life's turbulence if he/she was not at the helm? But my analyst's tone was an indicting one. So, as I lay down to free associate, I was especially attuned to compliance. To be deemed analyzable was my desire.

As I lay down on the couch, my analyst was outside of my view. In front of me on the otherwise blank wall hung a black and white photograph. Three winsome, pensive, latency-age little girls looked out at me with a perpetual curiosity, tinged with sadness. If I turned my head to the right and gazed downward, I could see my analyst's foot. There was much in the dressing and movement of that foot within which to fill the otherwise blank screen. For several months I spoke to the girls and my analyst's foot to the accompaniment of my analyst's supportive vocal utterances that said, "I'm listening, continue."

After a few months of my compliant talking, I was declared analyzable. I had begun to acquire some ease with this way of being together when my analyst interrupted her supportive "yes's" and "Mhmh's" to offer me an interpretation. I felt judged and a little shocked that her receptive listening would be used to shape a knowing pronouncement about me. Her interpretation settled over me like a web. I timidly began to protest to wrest myself from the gossamer-like envelopment of her words. She interrupted my verbal protest to offer yet another interpretation. Gently, but firmly she said, "You are experiencing me as critical and attacking. I am not that person. I don't know yet who in your past treated you that way. It is your past with significant others that leads you to see me as critical and attacking."

Thump. I understood in that moment: my analyst was (1) an authority on what was actually going on with me; (2) knew what was wrong with me; (3) knew that it was all within me; and (4) knew that it was determined by my past. I was relieved to know that someone knew and that the disturbance was within me. If it was in me, *I* could change. There was hope.

Her responses to me were determined by a set of rules that defined psychoanalysis. Neutrality, abstinence, anonymity, and verbal interpretations, among other ways of being, determined my analyst's response. Her manner in delivering her interpretations was infused with warmth and concern for me. However, any touching, extra-analytic contact, or my analyst's sharing of her experiences or feelings was clearly beyond the bounds of the analysis. These possible responses were beyond the bounds, not because my analyst chose to be a distant or withholding person, but because a critical component of cure within this theory required the analyst's abstinence. Freud stated it this way, "Treatment must be carried out in abstinence . . . The patient's need and longings should be allowed to persist in her, in order that they may serve as forces impelling her to do work and to make changes" (Freud, 1915, p. 164).

I understood the rules. I attended all of my sessions, arrived and paid on time, and spoke what came to mind. I asked nothing from my analyst outside of the hour. I gained increasing ease with speaking without conversational expectations, following more an intrapsychic train of thought. As my analyst listened and interpreted, she implicitly imparted permission to me to feel within the relationship and to give verbal expression to those feelings. My feelings and associated memories broadened and deepened. This process began to erode my capacity to remain emotionally removed in other relationships.

One Friday afternoon, in my fourth year of analysis, I met my mother for lunch. I greeted her, immediately sharing my exciting news. After being a full-time, stay-at-home mom for 8 years, I had decided to return to school. "Mom, I have been accepted into the Masters Program that I really wanted." "Congratulations," she responded immediately. "I am so proud of you." As I warmed to her celebratory praise, she continued talking. Sadness settled around her eyes and a slight tone of regret crept into her voice. She sighed, "Seems you always get what you want. You were like that when you were little too. Always had to be the best." She drifted into her own reverie, not exactly talking *to* me, and her regret had turned to resentment. "It was so hard on your little brothers." She paused, and then her gaze returned to me. "Can you even imagine what it has been like for your brothers, having to grow up with a sister like you? They never felt like they could do anything because you always had to be the best." My usual ability to neither hear nor feel the sting of my mother's words was confusingly absent. As I sat in stunned silence, her vituperative rant gained in intensity, "I don't understand why you didn't ever help your brothers. You always were helping others. Volunteering your time. A real do-gooder, but wouldn't help your own brothers. Others first, family second, that was always you."

My mother's familiar way of relating to me began to have an unfamiliar impact on me. A lifetime of these comments, comments that I had not really heard, now all pressed to be heard at once. The ensuing cacophony was dizzying and suffocating.

Later that night, 7:30 pm, my mother's shrill voice still echoed in my mind. Her words from earlier in the day continued to intrude and accuse, each one a sharp dart that pierced and shattered my sense of myself. "Selfish, hurtful, always." I tried to slow down my breathing. I tried to challenge the rationality of my mother's accusations. I tried eating. Finally, I paged my analyst. I had to talk to her. I needed her to listen and help me silence these annihilating words. My analyst returned my call and listened quietly as years of guilt, shame, and anguish dissolved into my tears. "Had I irreparably injured my brothers? How had being me hurt them, hurt her? Was I really a selfish, self-aggrandizing bitch?"

My analyst heard my mounting panic and urgency. I needed her presence. Her listening had begun to have its calming effect when I felt a shift in her compassionate silence. I felt a tension now in her listening. She wanted to end the call. I was too overwhelmed at that moment to comply with the demand that was implicit in her tense silence.

I had become in that moment a difficult patient. Uncharacteristically, I pressed on. My words continued to tumble at a rapid, unregulated pace. Thoughts were lost to me. I felt the strain of breathing and of my pounding heart.

I could feel her caring in her withdrawal, but she held her theory with strong conviction. To respond to my needs in the moment was to gratify my unconscious drives and thereby compromise my cure, she believed. My analyst finally interrupted. She spoke at a calm, measured pace, but with an authoritative tone that allowed no protest, "I will see you at our regular time on Monday. We will make a difference with these feelings for you."

Our regular time? *63* hours from now? I was enraged. My analyst's leaving me alone at that moment was more frightening and more disorganizing than my mother's earlier castigation of me. Then, all feeling drained away: life-saving non-life ensued. I found the calm of numbness, the numbness needed to avoid chaos. I understood in that moment as my analyst ended our telephone call that I would be expected, again, as when I was little, to endure unbearable feelings, all alone. I could not, would not, tolerate a process that would necessitate experiencing abandonment by the one from whom I expected care. I also feared that I had become a difficult patient, as my analyst had predicted I might.

From my analyst's theoretical perspective, she felt she needed to bear the tension of rejecting my demand for her presence. *I*, her difficult patient, was demanding a response that *she* knew would compromise the outcome of the treatment. On the other hand, her theory did allow for making certain provisions, breaking the analytic frame, if the patient were struggling. I imagine that such was her reasoning when she called later that evening to ask how I was doing.

With the tranquility that accompanies determination to leave a traumatizing relationship, I responded to her, "I am fine." She asked, hesitantly, "So you are doing better? I will see you on Monday?" "Yes," I replied tersely. I hesitated, and added, "but I will not be there on Monday. Since our earlier call, I have realized a few things. There will be a letter for you in your office on Monday." I moved to hang up. "That sounds ominous," she replied quickly. I felt the protective certainty of my decision to terminate challenged. I paused, "I do not mean it to be threatening, I just will not be back. I will place the envelope under your door." She then asked, "Would you meet with me at my office tomorrow morning instead of sending me this writing?"

I uttered a meek assent, but my feelings did not match my tone. Her response dissipated my lifeless state, but intense, too intense, feelings rushed in. Surprise and pleasure commingled with fear. I felt relief as the 61 hours now would only be 12, and she had responded. I felt confused and anxious as the serenity of the certainty of my decision to leave analysis was threatened.

As I drove to my analyst's office on that Saturday morning, I mentally rehearsed my words of termination to steel myself against any persuasive protests that I imagined she might offer. As I entered her office, she asked that we talk face to face. She explained to me that I was experiencing a confusion that was interfering with my treatment. I had confused her with my mother. She patiently explained that as we work in analysis I might experience her *as if* she were my mother, but that it was critical that I hold on to reality. She said, "I am not your mother. I am your analyst. We should meet face to face for the next several sessions to resolve the psychotic transference."

Thump. Again. I thought that I was angry with *her*. It was she who refused to be there for me, as I needed her. Instead, I am psychotic? I was stunned and more than a little mystified. I had forgotten what I had learned from her at the beginning of the analysis. It is all me, and in me, and *she knew* what was in me. After a few sessions where we sat face to face to dilute the intensity of my transference, I calmed down. I lay down again to understand more, and resumed my "as if" experiencing with my analyst. Her difficult patient again became a compliant patient.

At that moment, on a Friday night so many years ago, I became a difficult patient. I was difficult not so much because it was Friday night, after hours, after a long week, and I was difficult not so much because I demanded an emotional, personal response, but I was difficult primarily because the particular response that I needed was one that my analyst's theory deemed an impediment to the curative process.

Though today I would say that I actually was angry with *her* for not responding to me in a moment of crisis, I would add that her seeing me on that Saturday provided me with the requisite, healing response, despite, to me, the inaccuracy of the verbal content of her interpretation and her explanatory theory.

However, several years later, I moved from the analytic couch to the analyst's chair. As analyst, I began to question the objectivity and scientific truth of my former analyst's theory and her technique shaped thereby.

In my second analytic tale, specificity theory informed my therapeutic relationship with my patient.

Practice That Privileges Specificity of Process

The course of this analysis had been marked by rapid, extreme, and seemingly discontinuous shifts from positive to negative transference.[2] In the positive transference, my patient, Beth, experienced me as all good and powerful. She called me her "Jesus with skin." At other times, Beth perceived me as a sadistic seductress creating intimate, loving moments in order to enhance my power to injure her. And at still other times I was experienced as a neglectful therapist, turning away just at the critical moment when she needed comfort or protection. Beth's perception of me could alter rapidly, shifting from feeling safe with me to feeling either abandoned or even abused by me. And I need to add that these shifts would occur with little awareness on my part of any actual precipitant. To me, I might have felt only a slight alteration in my actual physical posture or expression, or warmth in tone or content of my speech.

This analytic tale begins toward the end of the third year of the analysis: There had been a tension between Beth and me perhaps since the earliest days of our work together. This tension had played at the edges of our relationship. We would feel it and flee from it, yet never fully acknowledged it, or name it. However, in this session, Beth was obviously upset as she entered my office.

Beth lay on the couch in silence. Her frustration and anger were palpable, as was my increasing tension and confusion. In the silence, I mentally reviewed our last session, and I could not recall anything that would now account for her feelings, something that might help me make sense of Beth's accusatory anger. She finally spoke, demanding, "Will you or will you not . . . hold me?" For me, the relational tension of this moment was crystallized, not by Beth's stark demand to be held, but in the vulnerability of her anguished plea, "I have to get the holding and soothing touch from you. This is too much for me to sit in your presence, the presence of caring. *I just actually need the physical touch.* I need to be held."

I expect that my body and facial expressions answered her question in the negative before I could even begin to think about her demand. In general, in my personal life, I am not a very touchy-feely person. I readily touch and hold my loved ones in order to comfort, reassure, or convey love. For a time. But I am not comfortable with holding or being held over time.

In deciding how to respond to Beth, I do not want to simply say "No." Rather than say, "No" or even "I don't know," I hope to stay with her feelings and convey my understanding, an understanding that might provide for her an *experience* of being held by me. "As you feel your love for me and mine for you, the old feelings of the baby not held or caressed come right along with them. Your suffering today from this early deprivation can only be relieved through my physical holding. Does it help when I understand and try to stay connected with the little one, connected through our daily voice mail exchanges?"

Beth turns away from me, from my implicit "no." I remain quiet. I can feel the intensity of her suffering, a pain that has been intensifying over the last several months, a pain that does not remit at the end our sessions. I feel, too, her painful confusion that her need of me creates for her. The mature, intelligent and competent adult craves being caressed and rocked as if she were an infant. I strain with the dilemma, a simultaneous desire to respond to and to retreat from Beth's plea.

Without a formal prescribed response found within most structure theories, I am left to engage in a unique analytic process with this patient. I must examine my own capacities and limitations to respond to my patient's demand, and explore the therapeutic implications of my response. Should I satisfy my patient's felt need, which feels uncomfortable for me, or endure my patient's disappointment, anger, and pain as I feel that I cannot provide the desired response, all within the context of how my responses might or might not be therapeutic for my patient. Without a predetermined theoretical answer or even guideline, I am called upon to analyze and assess my patient's demand upon me within the unique context and relationship that is always emergent between us.

Finally, Beth responds. "Your responsiveness makes these feelings more intense, but more manageable, too. I can talk about this forever, say the same thing forever. But it doesn't change the need to be held by you. *I want to feel you. My desire to be held needs to be satiated.* I am crying and crying to be fed, and you offer me words. Your words don't touch me."

This session initiated many more sessions that moved inevitably to her insistent demand to be held and caressed by me. My understanding of her agonized state deepened as I encouraged Beth to share her feelings, and her memories. Beth was born to a mother who had been too overwhelmed and depressed to respond to Beth. Her mother recounts today of Beth as a baby, she had been such a good baby, content for most of the day alone in her playpen. Beth recalls how she ached to be held, even putting her own small arms around herself, pretending that they were her mother's. She remembered many nights of her childhood where she hugged the plaster wall adjacent to her bed. After awhile the wall absorbed and held her warmth, and she could pretend that she was cuddled up to her mother.

When Beth was 2 years of age, her father's anxiety disorder had become so disabling that he was placed on leave from his job. With her mother's return to work, Beth's care was entrusted to her mentally ill father. Her father would lure her into shared delightful moments of intimacy, to startle, frighten or actually injure her. One such model scene (Lichtenberg, 2005) is captured in her memory of a cold winter night when she was 4. Her father awakened her from sleep to invite her to "Come. There is magic outside." He bundled her up in his large parka, enveloping her head to toe. He carried her outside. He whispered to her, "Now for the magic show," as he lifted the arm of the jacket, like a telescope. From within the dark, warm jacket she lifted her gaze and a sparkly starry sky magically appeared. She recalls the sudden thrill and shared excitement, as her father surreptitiously poured a glass of ice water down the sleeve. She fled, sobbing, wet and cold to the sound of his satisfied laughter. The others in the family chided her for being unable to take a "joke." Her mother not only was unable to be emotionally responsive to her little daughter, but she also did not protect Beth from her father.

However, my understanding and our deepened understanding of her feelings, through these revealed memories, did not ameliorate the intensity and torment of her desire to rest in my arms. We continued to explore her desire, and elaborate the possible meanings and genesis of this need and desire. We worked in this way for many months, but with each new understanding or memory, she would return to her concrete need to be held. She became desperate. She began to make plans to leave the analysis to find a therapist who would hold her throughout sessions. I felt a continual strain, and was regularly preoccupied with whether and/or how Beth and I would find a way to address her intensely felt need, a need that I could not actually satisfy.

Had this analysis been conducted with a structure theory, such as classical theory, I would have had a theoretical guide, even an answer. Freud provides the following answer to my dilemma: "Analytic treatment should be carried through, as far as possible, under privation . . . in a state of abstinence" (1919, 162). The analyst must ensure that "the patient is left with unfulfilled wishes in abundance" (1919, 164).

In other words, Freud prescribed abstinence. Abstinence was the assumptive stance, and any deviation therefrom, constituted a "provision." A provision (such as touching, let alone holding my patient) was anything other than interpretive explication, and was proscribed. A provision according to this theory would gratify my patient's unconscious libidinal wishes, depriving her of the opportunity to have them made conscious. Cure in this theory occurs as the unconscious libidinal strivings are made conscious and interpreted. With this new awareness, renunciation of the infantile wishes and replacement with more mature desires and goals becomes possible.

It is not only within classical theory that touching is prohibited. Most traditional psychoanalytic theories proscribe touch, let alone holding, as detrimental to the patient's healing. However, I work from the perspective of specificity theory, a process theory. Any particular clinician who uses this theory may or may not actually follow the theory's conclusion (indeed, as Freud himself did not always follow the dictates of his own writings on technique), but regardless of how a particular clinician may use the theory, I am concerned here with the operation of the theory itself. Specificity theory does not interdict touching (or any other response) unless it is illegal or officially proscribed by one's professional organization, but directs the analyst to engage with the patient to find out whether such a demand would be therapeutic for the patient and possible for the analyst.

My patient demanded, and believed, that her healing required my sustained, loving caress. However, my capacity to offer this response was limited, and fell far short of the holding that my patient craved. For me, holding has no natural or agreed upon stopping point. I imagined that I might begin to feel anxious over time with the physical or emotional containment that holding would require of me, which she would feel and possibly interpret as rejection. If we decided that I would hold her throughout the session, I imagined awkward discussions to determine the when and length of holding. Or would it become a ritual, the expected way that we would be together in session? With extended holding I imagined limbs going numb and itches left unscratched. How would we talk about *not* holding for a session, and what present and historical meanings would attach to such a discussion?

Further, and more significantly, given the nature of our relationship over the course of the analysis, the extended holding presented the danger that she would begin to feel that I was exploiting or abusing her. Two people experience and share intense feelings through physical holding that may be difficult to identify or talk about. Their meanings can be implicit, intense and rapidly shifting. Who is holding whom, who needs to be held, do I need her to need me to hold her? Throughout our relationship, Beth experienced me as abusive and exploitive whenever we felt increased intimacy. She was not able to explore these beliefs as her subjective experience, but rather as concrete proof of my malevolent intentions.

I was challenged to discern the response or responses that would provide healing experiences for my patient, and that I felt willing and able to provide. She began to experience my refusal as sadistic, that I had from the inception designed our interactions so as to create this intense need of me in order to enjoy my power to deprive. Or, alternatively, when she was experiencing me as less evil, she felt that my refusal was motivated by my own unconscious desire for her: It was I who desperately needed her, who needed her to be dependent on me. She reasoned that if I held her, she would gain health so that she no longer required therapy. I would then lose her, the one whom *I* so desperately needed.

As I continued to offer my patient my understanding and to undergo suffering with her, and to endure her resentment and anger, I came upon a blanket. It was of a size, heft, and texture that would envelope an adult as a parent would as she held a child. One side was made of a smooth satin that offered a rich, sensual tactile experience, and the reverse was made of a synthetic knit that offered a warmth, depth, and yield to the touch approximating the touch of a human body. I thought that it was possible that the blanket, if it were from me, might provide her with the needed experience of holding.

I wondered whether I should provide this concrete, demanded response. Should I have concluded that my difficulty with providing sustained holding imposed a debilitating limitation on therapeutic possibility in our work and help her find another therapist that worked in a different way than I? Or should I continue to try to respond, now, in this way? Would the comfort of the blanket so soothe that the experiences that gave rise to the unremitting pain no longer be available to the analysis, creating a kind of crippling dependency upon me for continual soothing? Or would it provide a response that would enable her to experience a relational world where loved ones respond to her pain without a desire to injure or exploit her. Or could it be experienced as both a healing response and, for a time, a needed level of dependency? These were the main questions I struggled with as I considered the possible therapeutic effect—or not—of this specific response—which I felt I *could* offer Beth.

As I presented the blanket to Beth in session, I asked "How would it feel if I were to give this blanket to you from me?" Beth was quiet, did not answer, and did not engage with me. As the session neared the end, she wordlessly picked up the blanket.

I awakened the next morning to a voice mail: "You are an analyst. So you can analyze me, but that is for you. I want you to know that the blanket . . . It is the coolest, smoothest texture. You were with me last night. I held the blanket tight and it brings me comfort. No panic attacks. You thought of the idea and it is working beautifully."[3]

Beth was able to use the blanket in other ways to regulate our relationship. When she was angry or disappointed with me, she was able to use the blanket to give more full expression to her feelings. The morning after a stormy session, Beth left me this voice mail: "With the blanket, I have improved my soothing mechanisms because I have you. But now I see that it helps because I can also have my way with you. You are not in that blanket so I am freer to have my way with it. It is safer than actually having you. It is full of life, yet lifeless. I don't trust. I am willing to try, but I know that I need some deep things, and I don't trust letting you close."

And then the blanket had a surprising negative effect. The blanket so perfectly matched her need and desire that it intensified her belief that I knew perfectly her private thoughts, beliefs, and feelings. "It is like you are God and you know me fully." This belief in my omniscience constrained our relationship. Now, if I acted in ways that were injurious to her, she could only believe that I did so with intention, as she knew that I knew perfectly what she wanted or expected. Further, during our sessions, if I inquired how she might feel about something, she became enraged, as she believed I knew how she felt. There was no reason to inquire, as I was all knowing, other than to delight in my power to injure.

Ultimately, the provision of the blanket did enhance Beth's trust in our relationship, and did provide her with an experience that seemed to contribute to an expansion of her ability to tolerate feelings and memories, and later to benefit from verbal interpretations.

My experience in this analysis, however, does not support either the offering of a blanket, even this type of special blanket, as a prescribed or even recommended response. Perhaps, I will never use a blanket in this way again. Nor does this analysis support the theory that allowing for parameters (Eissler, 1953) later permitted the *more ameliorative* verbal interpretation. Perhaps, my understanding as demonstrated through the offering of the blanket was essentially transformative for this patient even absent future interpretations.

In one session, months after the blanket had assumed its complex place in our relationship, Beth shared, "The angry, isolated place that I have been. It has felt like fighting the world, and now I see it is me. It is because of my trauma. My father was an ill man. He was abusive and sexually very twisted, and I was, am, sensitive, sensual, feeling, and I was left in his care full time. Physically, I had no soothing. I could scream. I could cry. Momma was tense and nervous. There was no calm holding. What I know of being comforted, I have learned through you. I now know that a baby has needs. Those needs need to be tended to and there is no shame. It is as simple as a baby needs to be held and comforted."

These two stories exemplify certain clinical contrasts and differing consequences between the utilization of specificity theory as process in contrast with a structure theory—such as Classical Psychoanalysis—a topic we address in depth in chapter 7. In the first example, the analyst's theory prescribed certain ways of responding and not responding to her analysand. The constraints of her theory—which, one might argue, had become a central part of who she was, professionally—determined her response and intimately shaped the nature of the relatedness between analysand and analyst. In the second example, with a theory that explicitly expands the range of therapeutic responsiveness non-prescriptively, theory played a different role in the therapeutic process and influenced therapeutic possibility in a fundamentally different way. It brought to the fore an examination of the particular way that *this analyst* might or might not be able to work optimally with *this particular patient*. That is, working with this theory required the analyst to examine possible limitations on *her capacity* to respond therapeutically to this *particular* patient. She was discovering, in process, how she could be, therapeutically, with this patient. She also creatively discovered a way of connecting with her that she could manage, at a symbolically archaic level, and that worked for her patient. Her own limitations and capabilities vis-à-vis this patient were at the center of her examination rather than theoretically defined standards, or structurally defined theory, against which to assess the patient's treatability (see also chapter 8, where we look more closely at the question of "analyzability" from the perspective of specificity theory).

Practice informed by specificity theory centrally entails a process of discovery of responses that may be therapeutically effective for a particular patient, without the use of prescriptive or proscriptive guidelines, whether or not the hypotheses of traditional structure theories usefully emerge. When we actually grasp the uniqueness and specificity of each therapeutic encounter, we are continually engaged in the moment to determine each time what is the needed therapeutic response, and what is possible for us to provide.

Specificity theory is a contemporary psychoanalytic process theory that is consonant with Gerald Edelman's theory of the uniqueness of the human brain and of the human mind as formed and created through ongoing selective interactions with its self, its environment, and others. In the next chapter, we consider in some depth the relevance of Edelman's view of brain function for specificity theory. At this point, though, we would emphasize that, given this bias of human creation, specificity theory as a theory of therapeutic efficacy exhorts the analyst to hold in mind the consequence of the reality that, at the level of theory, no one psychoanalytic structure theory can explain our patients nor determine our response. And at the level of clinical practice, therapeutic effect becomes determined by the limitations and capacities of each particular analyst and analysand to understand and respond to each other at any moment in time over the course of the analysis. In other words, the efficacy of each therapeutic endeavor is centrally a function of the specificity of fit of the participants in their interaction.

Specificity-fittedness

In our clinical experience, the "fit" is an especially important determinant of whether effective treatment is possible between the particular participants in the therapeutic venture. We have repeatedly discovered that the specificity of fit[4] of the treatment dyad has not been accorded the significance it deserves; in effect, the degree to which this capacity obtains between the participants within any particular treatment dyad may be fundamentally significant for the outcome of treatment.

Undoubtedly, many psychoanalytic therapists have intuitively practiced on the basis of what we now systematically conceptualize as specificity theory, simply because it makes good clinical sense. In other words, they "use" a process theory of therapeutic specificity as we understand it, perhaps much of the time, without recognizing or/and acknowledging that they are doing so.

In retrospect, and quite remarkably, my first inkling of such a practice—though I was yet to conceptualize it as such—was likely in my first class on the work of Melanie Klein at the British Institute of Psychoanalysis some 48 years ago. Elliott Jacques, the senior Kleinian analyst who was leading the class, told us, "You know, there are as many differences between how members of the Kleinian group at this Institute work with their patients as there are between the members of the Freudian and the Kleinian groups as a whole." It seemed to me at the time that this was the most unbelievable statement that an analyst at that Institute could make. I was not only incredulous, but wondered about his motives for making this assertion, suspecting that this was his—somewhat disingenuous—way of trying to mollify possible partisan tensions within a class that was composed of students whose allegiance belonged to the Freudian and Middle Group as well as to the Kleinian group. This may well have been the case, but I have come to recognize a deeper wisdom in what Jacques told us. He was, in effect, referring to *the specificity of dyadic process*. He was alluding to that part of process to which the analyst contributes, that is, that we bring so much more of ourselves to the interactions with our patients than our formal psychoanalytic theories, that the impact on the treatment of who the therapist is can supercede the influence of any formal theory.[5]

The absence of a theory of therapeutic specificity has left creative therapists vulnerable to the fear of being accused by their colleagues or by their own internal analytic police of practicing "wild analysis," of fostering an irresponsible ethos of an "anything goes" way of practicing. A reviewer of a paper on specificity theory submitted for publication in a traditional American psychoanalytic journal protested, "You might as well be giving dance lessons!" *Specificity theory does, in effect, hold that all potentially therapeutic responses in the treatment situation are legitimately utilizable—with the proviso that they not interfere with the therapist's professional functioning or exceed either the therapist's or the patient's personal tolerance.* Yet, the task of discovering responsiveness that is of optimal therapeutic value for the particular patient requires a high level of self-discipline and self-awareness, as well as familiarity with the concepts of traditional theory. In contrast to assuming that such and such a theory "goes with" the patient, attuning from moment to moment to what might be the most therapeutic response and, concomitantly, to consider whether one is able to offer it to that patient, is anything but "anything goes"; it is, rather, what being a good therapist is about. We must continue to examine whether our response was helpful, and to alter our responsiveness as best we can. Specificity theory recognizes that the specific responses that may be therapeutic are always in process.

The basis of the therapeutic power of the specificity of process lies within the biological architecture of the brain and a new theory of mind, which are the subjects of our next chapter.

NOTES

1. There are many philosophical and scientific perspectives on "emergence." Ours is in accord with Bedau and Humphrey's (2008) view that "Emergence relates to phenomena that arise from and depend on some more basic phenomena yet are simultaneously autonomous from that base" (p. 1), and that "emergent properties are 'novel' and 'unpredictable' from knowledge of their lower-level bases . . ." (Kim, 2008, p. 129).

2. This case was presented in conjunction with a co-authored paper by Howard Bacal and Lucyann Carlton, titled "Specificity Theory: Discovering Therapeutic Efficacy in the Specificity of Process," at the winter meetings of the American Psychoanalytic Association, January 20, 2008.

3. While this patient's use of the proffered blanket shares some characteristics of Winnicott's concept of the Transitional Object, it differs significantly in that this blanket was not "found" by the "infant" (Winnicott, 1971b).

4. Robert Stolorow actually suggested "specificity-fittedness" to me, as a more apt designation of what I meant by "optimal responsiveness." The term, "specificity-fittedness," has also been employed by Sander and by the Boston Change Study Group.

5. While I retain some uncertainty that specificity theory could in practice be utilized by Kleinian analysts, as their theoretical system is notably "closed," my supervisory experience with Wilfred Bion, a Kleinian icon, remarkably demonstrated this possibility. Despite Bion's apparent loyalty to Klein's theories, his clinical perspectives—and also his own theory of therapy (see Bion, 1967)—were imbued with a radically open systems approach to his patients.

4

The Neurobiological Substrate of Specificity Theory

FROM INSTRUCTIONIST MODELS OF THE BRAIN TO BIOLOGICAL SYSTEMS THEORY AND ITS IMPLICATIONS FOR PSYCHOANALYTIC THEORY AND PRACTICE

Historically, psychoanalysis moved away from Freud's early interest in the neurobiology of the mind to the phenomenological, subjective, and experience-near data of the clinical encounter. However, with the strides made in investigation of both the structure and function of the brain over the past twenty years, interest has been renewed in the brain-mind connection. Inquiry into and study of the internal processes of the mind has intensified within all the psychological sciences from developmental, cognitive, social, and behavioral psychology. There was a renewed interest in the covert, yet essential mechanisms that underlie overt behaviors. This expanded interest in the brain-mind connection has arisen within psychoanalysis as well. Theorists such as Allan Schore (2003), Daniel Siegel (1999), and Regina Pally (1998) began to link emerging knowledge of particular brain structure and function with creation of mind, to the interest of some and criticism of others (significantly Dr. Leslie Brothers [2002]).

The thinking seemed to go: animals are beings that seem to have a mind. So it is natural to make the assumption that a particular kind of biological organization would give rise to mental processes that would give rise to a mind. The predominant thrust of this theorizing was based upon "instructionist," or "constructionist," models. Predominant theorizing constructed computer models of brain function based on the assumption that such functions can be produced through computations and algorithms.

Researchers attempted to create model neural networks that acted upon information received from a simulated surrounding environment.

This chapter takes up the challenge that systems theory of life's origins and development poses for such models in psychoanalytic theory and practice—in particular, the far reaching implications of contemporary biological systems theory and the specificity of biological process for the creation, development, pathology, and cure of the human mind. The essence of these implications is that every human mind is unique, and does not form in orderly, definitive sequential stages with universal endpoints. There is no life form that exists as a somatic singularity; no life is ever a separate, self-contained, self-determining entity. Rather, from the moment of its creation and throughout its lifelong development, all life is formed and transformed within and as a part of particular ongoing systems relations of which it is one part and in which it is inextricably embedded.

As we have come to more fully apprehend that all biological life is formed through an ongoing, unique, dynamic creative process (see Edelman, 1992, 2004; Sander, 2002; Thelen & Smith, 1995; Thelen, 2005; Sacks, 1995; Lyons-Ruth, 2000; Tronick, 2003), our psychoanalytic theory and our practices must incorporate these qualities of development and change. The understanding that no life form could be studied or understood apart from its constituent systems has held revolutionary significance in all biological studies, but has yet to be systematically applied to the field of psychoanalytic theory and therapy: the study and treatment of the unique mind in interaction with that of the other.

The apparent simplicity of our initial descriptions of specificity theory thus belies a fascinating complexity that has its basis in cutting edge neurobiological research. Specificity theory is premised upon a biological systems approach that envisions every mind as unique and as continuously created and changed through ongoing interaction among mind, brain, body, and its particular environmental surround, human and non-human alike.

Gerald Edelman is the first, and yet only, scientist to offer a comprehensive mind/brain theory that attempts to describe brain function without analogies to the physical world, like engines or computers. Indeed, he asserts that brain function is far too complex to ever be reduced to computational models. Edelman contends, further, that the function and development of the brain, though subject to and dependent upon laws of physics, cannot be reduced to nor predicted by those laws. The questions and answers from physics are necessary, but not sufficient in the study of the brain. For Edelman, the matter of the mind must be approached from a biological point of view, not from a physical one. Edelman's thinking is premised upon the view that the mind is a special kind of biological process depending on special arrangements of matter. Edelman's findings are relevant not only for psychoanalytic theory in general; they affirm specificity theory's conceptualization of therapeutic process.

THE BIOLOGICAL STRUCTURING AND FUNCTIONING OF THE BRAIN

Edelman's work is voluminous and technical, and a comprehensive exposition of its complexity is beyond the scope of this book. The following is a simplified précis of Edelman's findings (see Edelman 1987, 1988, 1989, 1992, 1995, 1998, 2004).

Edelman emphasizes the primacy of the neuroanatomy of the brain, which preeminently establishes its uniqueness as an object and its functioning as a biological system. Edelman posits that the neuroanatomical structure and functioning of the brain are unique to each individual, and in each individual brain over time.

There is no single master plan for brain structure or function. It does not develop according to an external or even genetic master plan. There is no typology created from the top down. The brain is created from the bottom up by gradual selective processes, that is, through interacting and responding to its specific environment. No such idea exists in physics. Physical systems can be explained in terms of energy transfer, dynamics, causes, and even information transfer. There is no explicit information transfer between the environment and organisms. In biological systems, development works by selection, not instruction. There is no final cause, no teleology, and no purpose guiding the overall process. The response to the environment cannot be predicted beforehand, only observed after the fact.

Structurally, every brain is unique. Even in identical twins, neuronal structures are unique. No two brains are connected in the same way. Even in the same brain, the connections differ at any two different points in time. And neuronal connectivity is not exact; that is, it is not predetermined by a genetic code. It does not follow a blueprint. Connectivity is created as the brain develops through the three factors of development, experience, and reentrant connectivity. The brain is interconnected in a manner unlike any other entity. From the cellular level to the level of major pathways, all connections are three dimensional, and they shift. Edelman employs the term, "reentry," to describe the nature of the interconnectivity between individual neuronal groups, local maps, and global maps. Reentrant connectivity is not a simple linear connection where one neuron sends information to the other and in turn receives information from the other. It refers to a dynamic reciprocal type of connection where information flows both ways, but also continually alters the responses of the communicating neurons to increasingly achieve a state of integration of information and coordination of their activity, somewhat like the apparently chaotic yet responsively integrated playing of a skilled jazz ensemble.

It is true that, at the higher levels, the brain is organized into regions and specialized parts, but this fact does not support the conclusion that we can locate or understand any single function through its related specialized area. Edelman's model of global brain process has rendered the controversy in brain science of localization of function versus global process specious. The organization of the brain is characterized by *both*, that is both functional separation and specialization of neuronal groups and by global integration among the specialized functions. "Effective brain function arises both from the combined action of local segregated parts having different functions and from the global integration of these parts mediated by the process of reentry" (Edelman, 1998, p. 50). There is not a level of one to one correspondence as in computer-like linear communication. Rather, each function has many subfunctions (e.g., in the specialized area of vision there are more than thirty subfunctions such as detecting motion, color, and shape) and these functions are widely distributed over different brain regions. There is no central master area coordinating each disparate function yielding, for example, a single coherent visual image. These widely distributed functions interact and integrate to produce a single visual image through re-entrant signaling.

No two cells in the brain are alike. While cells within the same areas of brain specialization are more similar than two cells in different regions, no two cells are alike. Brain cells are formed with the potential to assume a vast number of specific functions. Neural function is, in Edelman's terms, "degenerate"; that is, neurons that are structurally different can perform the same function and the same neurons can perform different functions. The specific functions that a particular cell assumes are determined only a posteriori as it responds to, and interacts with, what Edelman apprehends as constraint values, or value systems in its particular environment (Edelman 2004; Edelman & Tononi, 1995), such as that particular brain's anatomy, neurochemistry, and electrical activity, the individual's history and level of development, health, etc. In other words, while the possibilities for the specificity of the brain's response are enormous, they are limited and regulated by the particular constraint values that may be present at any one moment in time. One example of such values, as Sacks (1995) points out, are experienced by the person as feelings. As the brain is thus created, it is not only a unique creation, but one specifically fitted to its unique environment. Edelman (1998, p. 45) calls this process "somatic selection," the analogue to "natural selection" at the creation and development of the individual person over the course of his or her individual lifetime.

That is, the brain, according to Edelman, "is a dynamic system that emerges from a selectional interaction with the world" (Edelman, 1998, p. 64). The brain has an enormous capacity for diverse responses to the environment (which includes both the physical environment and human surround).

Neuronal organization is premised upon "neuronal groups," as the brain functions and responds to its internal and external environment (Edelman, 1992, pp. 81–98; 2004, 32–47; Edelman & Tononi, 1995). As the brain interacts with its environment in "a kind of adaptive matching" that Edelman calls "recognition" (1992, p. 81), a specific response is selected. Through response to the environment, the brain is changed; the structure and function of the neuronal groups are altered and increasingly the brain becomes more fitted to its environment. While the brain is clearly a complex system, it is more; it is a complex biological *selectional* system. Edelman regards diversity as existing beforehand in a selective system and specificity arising as a result of selection ex post facto (see Edelman & Tononi, 1995; Edelman 2004).

IMPLICATIONS OF THE SPECIFICITY OF BIOLOGICAL PROCESS FOR PSYCHOANALYTIC THEORY AND PRACTICE

At the level of therapy, that is, of two minds interacting with each other, Edelman's view of the biological principles that inform somatic selection describe as well the process through which we can come to understand the unique and patterned way that therapist and patient come to be together, a type of "dyadic selection." This theory of the specific, interactive, and evolutionary view of all life creation matches exactly the process envisioned by specificity theory when applied to therapy. When two people come together there are vast potential ways that they might be together, that are shaped and delimited by the "constraint values" of who each one is with the other in specific context and environment to yield a specific therapeutic outcome that can only be understood after the fact. These limitations are, pari-passu, unique to the participants and to a particular point in time. Clinically, specificity theory captures Edelman's concept of constraint values by centrally recognizing that therapeutic effect is a function of the specific *limitations* as well as capacities of a particular dyad that emerge in the particularity of their process at any moment and over time.

If every brain is unique, and specifically fitted to its specific environment, Edelman's conceptualization of brain structure and function poses a fundamental challenge to psychoanalytic theories that rest on universals, structures, and typologies, and to prescribed methods of practice and responses that are based on such theories and prescribed methodology.

Adequate theories of brain, and a fortiori, mind, must incorporate variation and specificity.

The therapeutic relationship, in Edelman's view, is a biological nonlinear dynamic system (Edelman, personal communication, Feb. 2005). If this is so, an adequate psychoanalytic theory must incorporate characteristics of biological, nonlinear, dynamic systems. Specificity theory arises from the higher order "truth"—that is, the *fact*—that each of us is unique (that is, specific). Every person is unique and continuously being created, and specificity theory constitutes a higher order conceptualization of therapy that gives theoretical expression to that process.

Specificity theory is a process theory that envisions psychoanalytic therapy as a dynamic, unique system with unpredictable potential and limitations, consistent with characteristics of any living system as elucidated by Edelman. Specificity theory captures the uniqueness of mind and of relatedness that emerges from Edelman's model of the brain in recognizing the uniqueness of that therapeutic dyad and its potential for therapeutic effect at that particular time and over time.

Edelman's finding that brain function is, in effect, altered and created uniquely and specifically through, among other things, interactions with others, lends substance to specificity theory's questioning the appropriateness, or usefulness, of prescriptively applying the tenets of any structure theory. Theories that are premised on linear models of development, cause and effect relationships, internal representations, mechanistic or computational models are inadequate as they rest on principles that are incompatible with a biological selectional dynamic system that is the brain, mind, and minds in interaction with other minds.

Specificity theory's concept of mind as biological process is thus corroborated and deepened by Edelman's theory of brain function. Specificity theory does not reduce the mind to brain function in either a causal or correlative way (cf. Freud, 1895). Yet it is *consistent,* as all theories of mind must be, with our knowledge of the brain (Moran, 1991; Davis, 2002).

BRAIN-BASED EPISTEMOLOGY AND THE SPECIFICITY OF PROCESS

The articulation of a theory of specificity supports and enhances the therapist's capacity to engage in the essential ongoing process of discovering the specificity of her patient's mind, in interaction with her own mind, in each moment, and how this process might optimally play out for therapeutic effect. In his recent book, *Second Nature,* Gerald Edelman (2006) takes up the issue of Range and Specificity of Process. He reiterates throughout this book's exploration of a "brain-based epistemology" that the human brain has two modes of thought: pattern recognition and logic. Pattern recognition is the primary mode, the one first available to man and first available to each one of us at birth, and is the mode of thought available through primary consciousness. Pattern recognition permits rapid response to the enormously diverse environment to which man (and other animals with primary consciousness) must recognize and adaptively respond. The reduction of the environment's enormously diverse and complex features to a few recognizable generalized patterns enhances the automaticity of response and reduces the requirement for specific, conscious processing of the environmental stimuli and possibilities of response. In doing so, the brain trades specificity for range. Edelman avers (p. 102) that individual and species survival depends upon such a trade-off. Our primary thought processes are not rational, but metaphoric. The generalizations of pattern recognition are very adaptive, but to a point.

Secondary thought processes of logic permitted by higher order consciousness permit the individual to continue to process and interact with his environment to recognize the specificity within a general pattern. Secondary thought processes that recognize and incorporate specificity permit even more successful adaptation to an environment that is in fact specific. There are a number of brain mechanisms that enhance specificity, which include attention and conscious learning.

Applying this brain based epistemology to psychoanalytic theory would lead us to understand that our associational brains first and primarily generate generalizations to order and make sense of our world. Our brains tend to transform specific experiences into generalized patterns. That is, our brains continually generate patterns through which the world is known and interpreted and at the same time are amended and more specifically rendered through ongoing actual experience of the world.

Our structure theories are this type of metaphoric primary mode of thinking: articulating patterns of human development, health, and healing. While these theories provide generalities that enhance our range of recognition primarily through providing ordered patterns, they sacrifice specificity, which is present in all biological systems. These theories reflect how Edelman describes how our minds, striving for closure, tend to weave our world into conceptual wholes, or generalizations, so that the specificity of a constellation may be missed. In treating people, one size does not fit all, and we need a way to rise above the mind's inclination toward generalization and closure in order to discover what might be therapeutically relevant in particular instances. Articulation of a process theory of specificity helps the analyst to overcome the automaticity of pattern recognition and to sustain the tension that accompanies the much later acquired type of thought that searches for the specificity of the situation at hand within current process.

Put in another way, Edelman's research demonstrates that, neurologically, humans' consciousness creates an integrated seemingly seamless scene of the world (conceptual worlds as well as concrete worlds), which is not in fact a seamless whole (see Edelman, 2004, p. 136). We know that there are blanks and blind spots; we just are not able to hold such in awareness when we are actively engaged in creating a scene. So specificity theory reminds us to look and look again, recognizing that we will never fill in all the blanks nor discern all the critical elements to an interaction, and yet, at the same time, recognizing that our more rapid, initial impressions must be continuously challenged. Edelman demonstrates that the human mind seeks to make meaning of its world as it creates a meaningful world, and engages with the event/perception until it can make sense of it, when it becomes satisfied that this aspect of the world is "known." Specificity theory reminds us that, as curiosity diminishes, as one feels that one has achieved understanding—particularly in light of a structure theory—it may require additional effort to challenge and reengage the curiosity to search out other elements or meanings or even "unformulated theory" (see pp. 108–10 this book) to better apprehend the patient.

Louis Sander (1995) has noted that, "when we extrapolate to life's most complex level, the human mind, our designations of "mental representation," the "self," and "identity" can scarcely claim to be "structures" of static fixity, exempt from "process" (p. 583). As Carlton has noted, in concert with Edelman's findings and Sander's observations, the mind changes continuously in interaction with the brain, body, and environmental surround (human and non-human) as the person lives. Therefore, conceptual structures of the mind, such as id, ego, super-ego, RIGS, representations, internalized objects, poles of self structure or organizing principles, are only apparently fixed and immutable. They are always in process. Mind forms and functions in relationship with others, and is envisioned as able and open to change in surprising ways. Referring to the construction of rhythm in the non-linear dynamic system, Sander avers that "[E]ach recurrence of pattern [may] resemble previous patterns but is unique in its own way" (Sander, 2002, p. 22).

Specificity theory is a theory that explores, expands and applies our awareness of the therapeutic implications of an understanding of mind as always in process, emergent, and continuously created through relations with its many environments. There is no assumption of average expectable developmental unfolding through sequential stages, or predetermined universal end-state, and no assumed universal motivations. Every mind is unique and even unique from itself from moment to moment in time. Order is understood as emergent, and change is influenced by the ongoing interplay of system components (of which the analyst is only one) in unique and unpredictable ways.

The paths I took to reach this view began some time ago. I invite you to join me, in the next chapter, to trace my discoveries on the journey that shaped its development.

NOTE

This chapter comprises my edit of Lucyann Carlton's articulation (personal communication, 2010) of how Gerald Edelman's research on the structure and function of the brain applies to psychoanalytic theory in general and specificity theory in particular.

5

The Evolution of Specificity Theory: A Professional and Personal Odyssey

Stolorow and Atwood (1979) have persuasively argued that theoretical models in psychoanalysis and psychotherapy implicitly reflect their authors' life experience. In sharing aspects of my life that have contributed to the development of specificity theory, my intent is not only to confirm this, but also to model the Weltanschauung of the theory itself—that sharing about such influence on how we theorize and how we work can promote a better understanding of both. My intent is also to offer a model for training institutions in the teaching and learning of psychoanalysis and psychotherapy, a model that demonstrates a central postulate of specificity theory itself. The theory is premised upon the uniqueness of each of person, and of each potentially therapeutic and pedagogic dyad. Such uniqueness emerges from and becomes evident in our interactions with others, and it centrally influences therapeutic possibility and effect. If this is so, our life experiences and our relational history become variously relevant, and important, aspects of both treatment[1] and of education for doing psychotherapy.

In chapter 1, I described how my participation in an unusual psychotherapy outcome research project—research that incorporated specificity in its assessment methodology—stimulated my thinking about specificity in therapeutic process. This was just one of a number of experiences over time, both personal and professional, that evoked and shaped my interest in specificity in therapy.

A DIFFERENT PSYCHIATRIC RESIDENCY

My first encounter with challenges to traditional psychoanalytic thinking was during my psychiatric residency at the University of Cincinnati. The ethos within this department of psychiatry during the 1950s and early 1960s comprised a curious mixture of analytic traditionalism and eclectic psychodynamic perspectives.[2] We were expected to apply these precepts with our patients in psychotherapy, especially those of Freud's classical theories about sex and aggression and the Oedipus complex. But these concepts often did not feel relevant in understanding my patients or in responding usefully to them. What made more sense to me was an approach to the treatment situation introduced by the chairman of our Department, Maurice Levine, who had trained with Franz Alexander. As residents in training, we did not know that Alexanders's concept of the corrective emotional experience (Alexander, 1956) was censured by the traditional psychoanalytic establishment. We just found it useful clinically. Levine taught this concept as a way of creatively individualizing psychotherapeutic intervention. Insight mediated by interpretation was only one of the many ways that our patients could get better. While this approach made sense to me, it was at variance not only with traditional psychoanalytic theory and it application, but also with the traditional psychoanalytic assumption that verbal interpretive explanation is the only clinical activity that is truly mutative.[3] It was also different from what we were hearing from other members of our senior teaching staff who, for the most part, comprised qualified psychoanalysts: that the particular interpretive responses that formal psychoanalytic theory prescribed were the only ones that truly mediated therapeutic effect. Quite a mixed and confusing message; yet, interestingly, no one commented on it! The most pervasively powerful message on the street was, however—at least to my idealizing ears, as well as to those of a number of my fellow residents—that in order to really learn how to do depth psychotherapy effectively, one had to know what our teachers really knew. And there was only one way to acquire this knowledge: one had to become an analyst oneself, during which process one would undergo a personal analysis. So I planned to undertake psychoanalytic training. My choice at first seemed to be either to return to Canada to enroll in the first class of the new Canadian psychoanalytic institute, or to brave the notoriously critical assessors at the Chicago Institute for Psychoanalysis, where several of our teachers in the department of psychiatry at the University of Cincinnati had trained.[4] I then discovered another, adventurous, alternative: The Institute of Psychoanalysis in London, England.

ANALYSIS AND ANALYTIC TRAINING: MICHAEL BALINT, WILFRED BION, DONALD WINNICOTT, AND MARION MILNER

The perspective on treatment in Levine's department of psychiatry—that variability of responsiveness according to the patient's need was therapeutically appropriate—was not reinforced by the ethos of analytic training school. Most of those who taught theory—though fortunately not most of the supervisors I chose—knew, on the basis of *their* theories, just what should be done clinically with my patients. My experience in another sector of analytic training—personal analysis—reflected this view. On the basis of my analyst's theories about me, he knew who I was and what would be therapeutic for me.

At the British Institute of Psychoanalysis, where I trained in adult and child psychoanalysis during the 1960s, the first year of classes comprised a common course for all students, which focused mainly on Freud's writings. Subsequently, teaching was organized into three streams, corresponding to the work of psychoanalysts that reflected theories espoused by the three groups within the British Psychoanalytic Society—the Kleinian, Orthodox Freudian, and Independent, or Middle, Group. Prospective candidates were required to state in advance the course stream they would follow if they were accepted for training. This essentially meant joining one of the "groups." As I had not been especially impressed by the clinical applicability of classical theory, and had little idea what Kleinian theory was about—and in any case felt somewhat uneasy about orthodoxy—I elected to become affiliated with the Middle Group.

Students usually attended only the classes offered by one of the three groups with which they chose to be affiliated, but I was still interested in finding out more about all of them, so I attended as many classes as I could in all three streams. While I reacted (inwardly) when my teachers would effectively declare their perspectives to be "right," I also felt enriched by studying their differing truths, which I attempted to apply in my clinical work. Similarly, I selected supervisors for my adult and child "control cases" from all three streams, or "groups." Interestingly, most of my supervisors focused their observations on what seemed to be going on between my patient and myself in the analysis regardless of their strongly held theoretical views. I only ran into difficulty with authoritative canon when I experienced it being turned on me during my personal analysis; yet, in retrospect, my rebellion against this, in this setting, significantly catalyzed my interest in developing a very different theory of psychoanalytic treatment.

When you are a candidate in an analytic institute, your personal analysis is termed a "training analysis"; that is, it is a required component of the training, considered equal in importance to the other two—theoretical seminars and supervision. Consciously and/or unconsciously, a trainee-analysand tends to identify with his analyst's ways of working with him. This did not work very well, though, for me, with my analyst. My analyst's interpretations tended repeatedly to focus on what was wrong with me. I had significant difficulty utilizing this approach, both for myself and in therapeutic work with my patients. Remarkably, though, as I will soon describe, Michael Balint's supervision of my work with my training, or "control," case—within the analytic setting—was extraordinarily helpful.

From my analyst's viewpoint, I met the essential criteria of Freudian ill health. He consistently interpreted my associations as conclusive evidence that I didn't want to work and that I didn't know how to love. Even if there were a kernel of truth to his interpretations, I had no idea how to make use of them. Balint's interpretations, however well intentioned, felt like blows, blows that left me feeling helpless, ashamed, and enraged. I protested, as I had done as a child, to my first, unaccredited analyst—my bright, "knowing" mother—when she would label me with contemptible traits, in scathing tones, accompanied at times by physically hurtful blows. My father was of little help in this situation, as he seemed to be somewhat in the same boat I was in with my mother, and he did not even try to rock it, let alone provide a different sort of responsiveness to me. A kind and especially talented pediatrician, my father spent most of his time attending to the needs of his little patients and their mothers, who thought the world of him. So I found it terribly hard to disavow the truth of my analyst's views about how bad I was. It was only years after that analysis ended that I could effectively begin to disavow the validity of his pronouncements. They *had* to be true—because he (like my mother) knew—me, and what was wrong with me. It was years later before I could seriously consider whether these knowing pronouncements were true, and how well did he know—*me*?

Not only did my analyst's proclamations about me not feel good, what he was doing didn't feel quite right. In one session, I found myself imploring him to relate to me in a different way. Rather than hurl interpretations at me from up there, could we be like two children sitting on the floor side by side, leaning against the couch looking at something together and discussing what each of us saw in it? My intent with this metaphor was to elicit the sort of responsiveness that I felt would allow me to experience with him a sense of non-judgmental equality that could enable me to use the therapy. I think I was also trying to convey to him how we could be together so that he might get to know me in a different way, and that I might, in that way, even get to know him better, too.

This was, in retrospect, my first attempt at a *creative* solution to a lifelong impasse. In expressing my wish for some sort of "enactment" of a felt therapeutic need, I was not only challenging the "only way to work" in psychoanalytic therapy. I was also suggesting that there might be a better way that this activity called analysis could be carried out with *me*. I cannot remember his response at the time (which likely means that he said nothing). But I do recall how frustrating it was that he did not change how he went about "analyzing" me, and how distressing it was that I could not "change" my own sense of the validity of his opinions about me.

There was no one I felt I could talk to about this. In some desperation I drafted a paper, toward the end of that first year of analytic training, which I titled, "Is Analyzing Necessary?" (Not, "How Does Analysis Cure?" but, "Is Analyzing Necessary?")—my second incipiently creative attempt to draw attention to the therapeutic ineffectiveness of the way I was being "treated," along with suggestions for different ways of trying to be therapeutic. I assessed, probably wisely, though, that if I were to bring this little treatise to the light of day, I might not get much further in my analytic training school. I have in fact never written that paper but I have come to appreciate that its content contained the anlage of what specificity theory came to address, many years later. I have since wondered whether such specificity may have been a significant factor in Harry Guntrip's experience in analysis with Fairbairn, and then with Winnicott.

Fairbairn had developed a theoretical system that radically challenged that of Freud, yet Fairbairn conducted Guntrip's analysis in a strikingly classical mode, which did not enable Guntrip to engage archaic relational needs that Fairbairn's use of his own theories might have facilitated (see Guntrip, 1975).[5] Guntrip, in effect, subsequently got from Winnicott the kind of responsiveness in practice that Fairbairn espoused in theory. My experience in analysis with Balint was similar to Harry Guntrip's experience with Fairbairn. Balint, too, had developed innovative theoretical perspectives on treatment of patients in regression (Balint, 1937, 1968), yet my experience of his responsiveness to me was that of a maturity morality that did not at all include this understanding. Analogous to Guntrip's later more helpful analytic experience with Winnicott, I found a better fit with Heinz Kohut, which I will describe later in this chapter (also see Bacal, 2006).

Experience with certain supervisors also stimulated my thinking about the power of specificity in psychoanalytic practice. These pre-eminently included Michael Balint, Wilfred Bion, Donald Winnicott, and Marion Milner. Balint supervised my first analytic control case for seven and a half years according to the Hungarian psychoanalytic training system, wherein the training analyst supervised the candidate's first case within the candidate's own analysis,[6] as he shares his experience of his patient in the course of his associations. This experience was quite different than when Balint directed his understanding to me alone. I found this form of supervision to be immensely valuable, as it enabled me to appreciate, with striking immediacy, how certain aspects of who I was in context affected my responses to my patient. I was eager to begin my first analytic training case, under Balint's supervision; but I conveyed to him that I was also feeling curiously ambivalent about starting the work with the patient I had selected—an interesting but apparently "difficult" young woman who, I noted during my associations in an analytic session, was around the same age as my younger sister. My resistance started to fade when Balint interpretively inquired whether I was ready for a little sister. His interpretation derived from my having told him earlier that when my sister's nurse left when she was one year old, I (four and a half, at the time) was heard to ask why she was not taking the baby with her; after all, she had arrived with her! During another session, I anxiously conveyed to Balint that I was having trouble working with a certain patient, as she seemed to be uncomfortably like me in some respects. I was startled—but enormously helped—to hear him say, "Every patient is the same as every other, yet completely different." Now, with specificity theory, we would add, so is every therapist with every patient.

Not everyone who worked with Balint in this kind of supervision found it so useful. Some years after completing my analytic training, I learned from a fellow student who had also undertaken supervision with Balint in this way, that he found it quite noxious. Another interesting instance of the specificity of pedagogic and personal experience.

I not only appreciated Balint's supervision of my first training case in this way, I also valued his innovative theoretical thinking. Balint was unafraid of challenging hallowed assumptions if they did not fit clinical observation.[7] As early as 1939, Michael and Alice Balint had drawn attention to the analyst's influence on the development of the transference, which was a revolutionary idea at the time. Balint also observed that not everything the analyst experienced necessarily derived from the patient's transferences,[8] which also flew in the face of commonly held analytic theory of the time. Most analysts, then, also regarded verbal explication to be the sine qua non of proper analytic work, as many still do. Remarkably ahead of his time, Balint contended, as early as the late 1940s, that especially for patients in regressed states, it was the nature and quality of the relationship that was therapeutically central. He further asserted that "both the form and depth of regression [should be considered] as the result of an interaction between the *particular* patient and the *particular* analyst" (Balint 1968, p. 162) (italics added).

So, to an appreciable extent, I picked up the importance of relational specificity from Balint though, remarkably, he was much more inclined to recognize the usefulness of this between myself and my patients than between him and me. A curious situation, for which there are likely many determinants. I have wondered whether one of them was a psychoanalytic version of the familiar phenomenon of the heightened tolerance of the grandparent for his grandchildren than for his own children. In this context, the grandparent was Balint to his trainee-analysand's patients—that is, to my analysands. My analytic grandfather, in this context, was Sandor Ferenczi, with whom, I suspect, I might have experienced a more therapeutic fit.[9]

In yet another setting, I also learned from Balint about the importance of specificity of interaction for therapeutic effect. In addition to my involvement in psychotherapy research at the Tavistock Clinic, I led discussion groups at the "Tavi" for general practitioners in the psychological aspects of their work. These groups, which Michael originated and were further developed by Michael and his wife, Enid, also a psychoanalyst, strikingly illuminated the remarkably variegated ways that patients experience their doctors as therapeutic, and how particular doctors could or could not work effectively with certain patients (Balint, 1957, 1969; M. & E. Balint, 1961). These groups, which came to be called "Balint Groups," are a form of applied psychoanalysis (E. Balint, 1967). Their central task comprises the study of the therapeutic effect of the *particular* patient-doctor relationship. Balint held regular supervision meetings for psychoanalysts as part of their training to lead such groups, which still have a worldwide following under the aegis of the International Balint Society.

During a substantial portion of my supervision with Wilfred Bion, he was focusing on perspectives that he was writing about in his paper, "Notes On Memory and Desire" (Bion, 1967). In this paper, Bion recommended that the analyst expunge any prior knowledge or conception of the patient he is about to see, except his name and the hour that he is expected to appear for his appointment. I could never quite emulate this approach, but it impressed upon me the value of sustaining a truly not-knowing state of mind, and drew me more deeply into attending to the uniqueness of the patient as it impacted myself as the analyst.

Donald Winnicott and Marion Milner both espoused a clinical approach that richly foreshadowed that of contemporary relational self psychology (see Bacal, 1989; Bacal & Newman, 1990). Like Ferenczi, Winnicott also recognized—and conveyed to me—that what may be most important to the patient is not what the analyst interprets but how the analyst behaves. But there was still no theory for this—just clinical impressions, which were not aired at psychoanalytic meetings, only shared, perhaps, with close colleagues and sometimes with students. I remember Winnicott telling me, some time in 1967, how impressed he was with a young social worker that he observed treating a child when on a recent visit to New York. Had I heard of her, he asked? Her name, he told me, was Virginia Axline, and she had written a remarkable book, *Dibs, in Search of Self* (1964), in which she described the effective treatment of a child "without making any interpretations at all!" (Actually, it seems that she did, but this is not what impressed Winnicott about how Axline was therapeutic with her young patient).

Winnicott told me a similar story about Melitta Schmideberg, the physician psychoanalyst daughter of Melanie Klein, who had taken a job working with psychotic children at a mental hospital north of London shortly after the Klein family emigrated to England in the late 20s. "She knew not a stitch of English at the time," Winnicott told me, "yet her therapeutic effect on those children was amazing." I vividly recall the preliminary meeting I had with Winnicott when I was about to begin the analysis of a three-and-a-half-year-old girl under his supervision. The child's behavior had become chaotic and bizarre in the context of the meager one-room flat in which she lived with her father, her mother, and her two year old sister. I asked Winnicott how to begin the treatment (as I had never worked with a child before and had not a clue what to do). Without hesitation, Winnicott answered, "If she holds out her hand, take it." I have never forgotten this. It became not only a metaphor for the responsivity that enabled me to be therapeutic for my little patient—but for my work with adult patients as well.

I had similar experience of Marion Milner's daring to think quite differently about what a particular patient might need. During her supervision of one of my adult training cases, she understood my sensitive patient's retreat into the woods as a young adolescent, where he would lie for hours in holes he would dig in the ground, as a way to find him*self* and to grow. Milner suggested that I might apprehend that behavior as tantamount to the beginning growth of a delicate young plant that needs careful tending as it begins to sprout new shoots, rather than some kind of seriously schizoid withdrawal as previous psychiatrists and psychoanalysts had diagnosed. I think Marion Milner, along with Guntrip, must truly have been the first "self psychologists."

This sort of supervision of my patients was, understandably, also stirring a good deal of conflict in me about how analysis does cure, as my own analytic experience, which was going on at the same time, was quite different. It was to take me about twenty five more years before I truly appreciated that relational frustration in analysis was not going to be optimal for my personal development. It was only then that I could begin seriously writing about how I thought psychoanalytic treatment could be therapeutic (Bacal, 1985).

FROM OPTIMAL FRUSTRATION TO OPTIMAL RESPONSIVENESS

On my way toward developing specificity theory, my critique of the classical psychoanalytic assumption that frustration is intrinsic to treatment is understandable. My second experience of analysis, with Heinz Kohut, was very different, as I will soon describe, yet I found myself also critiquing a central facet of Kohut's theory of psychoanalytic cure, *"optimal" frustration*. In my critique, I questioned (Bacal, 1985) the axiom that experiences of either "gratification" or "frustration" were inherently relevant for therapeutic effect (Bacal, 1985). The former—gratification—had been regarded as antithetic to it, and the latter—frustration—to be necessary, in some degree (see Bacal, 1985).

Explicit in Freud's theories, and identifiable in many others since Freud's, is the prescription that treatment is to be carried out in "abstinence" (see also, Ricci and Broucek, 1998). It goes something like this: In order to ensure therapeutic effect, both participants must eschew gratification, and the analyst must subtly and also not so subtly, introduce a measure of frustration into the treatment.[10] Another stated rationale for this, from the perspective of classical psychoanalytic theory, is to enable unconscious phantasy to emerge into the transference (see Bacal, 1985, pp. 202–209). Ricci and Broucek (1998) have argued that the more or less official installation of frustration into the analytic process as pivotal to therapeutic effect may also—and perhaps predominantly—have been motivated by anxieties that the sexual tenets central to early psychoanalytic theory were threatening the respectability and viability of the movement

But it has not only been classical theorists who have emphasized the importance of frustration in psychoanalytic treatment. It is, interestingly, also intrinsic to how psychoanalysis cures according to Kohutian self psychology theory (1981). In the late 1970s, I became interested in Heinz Kohut's psychology of the self, in effect, his "selfobject theory" (Basch, personal communication) as it seemed to add an important theoretical and clinical dimension to the "object-relational theory" with which I was familiar, that is, the centrality of the "self's" experience in therapeutic relatedness (Bacal, 1987; Bacal & Newman, 1990). Kohut had developed two major theories of therapy: a theory of therapeutic cure and a paradigm for therapeutic action. According to Kohut (1984), "cure" comes about through experiences of "optimal frustration," that is, via the transformation ("transmutation") into self-structure of experiences of manageable frustrations in respect of the selfobject failures of one's analyst to be available for needed selfobject responsiveness.

Kohut also articulated a methodological paradigm for therapeutic action in psychoanalysis, which is applicable not only to self psychology theory but also to any of our familiar psychoanalytic structure theories. Kohut regarded therapeutic action in psychoanalysis as consisting of "two separate, identifiable, but interdependent steps, (1) *empathic understanding*, and (2) *explaining*" (1984, 94) (italics added). Most analysts would still essentially agree with this. For Kohut, empathy, or vicarious introspection, is the tool of data gathering, constituting the human capacities that make the investigation of the inner life of another possible. With his classical confreres, Kohut defined the second step of his formulation of the basic therapeutic act, the response, narrowly and singularly as explaining. Within the prevailing classical theory of his day, the only legitimate psychoanalytic response was to offer the results of the analyst's sustained empathic listening in a verbal formulation to and about the patient.

Kohut's second step in this paradigm for therapeutic action did not, however, accord with my experience either as analysand, analyst, supervisee, or supervisor. Rather, in all these areas, I felt I was experiencing what was obvious but curiously unobserved—and pretty evidently politically deviant to declare—that, in addition to interpretive explanation, patients variously experience a widely variegated responsiveness as therapeutic (see Bacal, 1985, 1998). To mention but a few: empathic attunement, the creation of a propitious therapeutic atmosphere, playfulness, humor, confrontation, support, (such as active encouragement, praise, or advice), sharing of the *analyst's* affects or subjective experience ("self-disclosure"), restraint, validation, or invalidation. A wide range of nonverbal experience, sometimes grouped under the rubric of "enactment" of various sorts, can have significant therapeutic effect. To name only a few of these: smiling, frowning, crying, touching, extra-analytic contact, or offering a blanket; receiving or giving a gift. Or taking a walk with the patient, which apparently Sigmund Freud did with Sandor Ferenczi long ago, and Frank Lachmann did with his analysand much more recently (see Ferenczi, 1909; Lachmann, 2010). Optimal therapeutic responsiveness for the patient may also entail his or her experience that he can affect the *analyst* in various ways,[11] for example, by offering understanding and admiration, or anger, or through caring and giving—a neglected area in relation to therapeutic effect that Ian Suttie recognized a long while ago (see Bacal & Newman, 1990).

Now, perhaps many—though likely not most—analysts would maintain that we always knew all this. Undoubtedly some analysts really have "known" all this; but this is different from acknowledging that they actually approach the psychoanalytic situation in this way. Such recognition is usually given sotto voce, shared, as it were, in hallways between trusted colleagues—"You won't believe what was crucial for this patient!!" (see Bacal & Herzog, 2003). *Yet there has been no theory for this way of working.* In the psychoanalytic world, the officially recognized curative response is interpretive explanation, against the backdrop of "optimal frustration." The position largely taken is that therapeutic effect results from reflective awareness according to the prescriptions of formal theories.

HOW *DOES* ANALYSIS CURE? BEYOND KOHUT'S TWO-STEP PARADIGM

Along with Terman (1998),[12] I offered another perspective (Bacal, 1985, 1998, etc.). I suggested that the concepts of frustration and gratification are irrelevant to psychotherapeutic work when they are used as generalizations and separated from the idea of responsiveness that is therapeutic for the particular patient—for which I offered the term, "optimal responsiveness." That is, this concept not only offered a perspective on therapeutic effect that was at variance with the assumption that frustration is ubiquitously central to analytic cure; it offered a different approach to the treatment situation and questioned the therapeutic relevance of any universally applied mode of responsiveness.

I first illustrated this in the context of broadening Kohut's second step in his paradigm for therapeutic action. I suggested that his second step—interpretive explanation—could usefully be replaced by the concept of optimal responsiveness (Bacal, 1985). Optimal responsiveness refers to a way of practicing that gives substance and accords legitimacy to the variegated spectrum of therapist responsiveness that patients may actually experience as therapeutic. In effect, with this concept, I broadened Kohut's second step of his two-step sequence of therapeutic action from interpretation, or explanation, to include an array of responsiveness that includes, but transcends, verbal explanation (interpretation) (see p. 50). The use of the term, optimal, also effectively implied that that no response can be deemed to be therapeutic without central regard to its relevance to the patient's *particular* therapeutic need. In other words, I was both critiquing and simultaneously addressing three problems posed by Kohut's clinical theorizing. The one was how cure comes about—that is, through "optimal frustration" and "transmuting internalization" (Kohut, 1984); the second was how Kohut saw this being implemented—through the second step of his two-step procedure for therapeutic action, which restricted the analyst's responsiveness to verbal explanation (interpretation); and the third was the lack of specificity with regard to what may constitute the optimal therapeutic experience for the patient that the analyst's response may mediate at any particular time.

The concept, "optimal responsiveness," is not intended to denote the "best" or the "perfect" response (one of the connotations of the word "optimal"), nor does it signify that "anything goes." On the contrary, the task of discovering responsiveness that is optimal is a systems concept that requires careful consideration from moment to moment about what might be optimal for the particular patient's therapeutic experience, and simultaneously finding out whether one is able to offer this. The particularity of the *analyst* is, in process, inextricably implicated in the responsiveness that she can optimally offer that patient. This way of viewing the complexity of the treatment situation was remarkably foreshadowed in Balint's view of therapeutic effect as comprising a system of "the doctor, his patient, and the illness" (Balint, 1956).

From the analysand's point of view, what will be therapeutic is the responsiveness from his analyst that he or she needs that moves his experience of treatment forward.

OPTIMAL RESPONSIVENESS IMPLIES A THEORY OF THERAPEUTIC SPECIFICITY

The concept, optimal responsiveness (Bacal, 1985, etc.), therefore, not only argues against the notion that there is always a degree of frustration that is central to analytic cure (though it does not assert that experiences of frustration cannot be productively catalytic), not only conceptualizes and legitimizes a widened range of therapeutic action, but also implies a radically different theory of psychoanalytic treatment: that the *specificity within psychoanalytic process is integral to when therapy happens or not.*

HOW KOHUT ACTUALLY WORKED—WITH ME

My second analytic experience, with Heinz Kohut, went much better than the first one. In the early days of my analysis with Kohut, I discovered, as a kind of revelation, really, the therapeutic power of empathy as response. Like many of my colleagues and fellow-analysands at the time, I had come from a prior analysis in which this way of talking to patients was not regarded as having very much use. In effect, it took me some time to get over experiencing Kohut's fairly consistent way of talking with me like this as somewhat indulgent; but it was useful for me, for a good deal of the time, though not always (see Bacal, 2006).

Kohut, at times, offered responses other than interpretation and empathy that I experienced as therapeutic. I am not the only one who benefited from Kohut's inconsistency in adhering to his declared two-step procedure for therapeutic action. There are two published examples of this that are quite striking. Perhaps the most famous one is that of Kohut's patient, Miss F—a case that is often cited as template for the discovery of self psychology (see Kohut, 1971, 283–290). Miss F was a patient for whom the echoing of her subjectivity was the only response she experienced as therapeutic; anything else provoked catastrophically self-disorganizing rage. Kohut could not help her for some time, as he was wedded to a way of working that prioritized conceptualizing and delivering verbal understanding, that is, interpreting. It was to Kohut's credit that he was ultimately able to shift from this mode to one of simply providing a mirror for her experience, which turned out to be remarkably effective. We note that Kohut's response to Miss F that was useful to her was neither that of interpretation nor empathy. The other—almost equally well known—example is that of Kohut's offering a patient two fingers to hold at the point when he feared she was becoming seriously suicidal (Kohut, 1981). Interestingly, Kohut tells us that as he did this and the patient took hold of his fingers, he made an interpretation—to himself—"[b]ecause an analyst always remains an analyst . . . It was the toothless gums of a very young child clamping down on an empty nipple" (ibid., p. 535). In fact, Kohut did not, in this situation, make an interpretation to the patient, nor was he offering his patient empathy as therapeutic response. But because analysts define themselves as analysts by virtue of their adherence to the belief, or doctrine, that only interpretation can "cure," an interpretation had to figure somewhere in Kohut's response, even if articulated silently. In effect, the action he deemed therapeutic was that of offering his two fingers for his patient to hold onto. Kohut understood via his empathic attunement to this patient that, for her, at this time, her *experience* of being apprehended (her experiencing his empathic attunement to her lifelessness) could not be mediated through his verbal expression of his feeling for her. The patient needed to experience Kohut's extension of himself and then the opportunity to hold on. Offering the two fingers was not an interpretation, but it did, in our view (see Bacal & Carlton, 2010b) constitute the practice of psychoanalysis at its best, exemplifying Kohut's ability to understand and move to the patient's therapeutic need. Our view (ibid.) is that it was also self psychology, specifically utilized, at its best. While Kohut's empathic understanding and associated response were informed by the structure of his theory, they were not limited by the constraints that would direct him to interpret the patient's archaic selfobject need rather than to provide it, symbolically, in this particular instance.[13]

My experience of analysis with Kohut leads me to conclude that he was not constrained, in practice, by the way he defined his two-step theory of therapeutic action. In fact, Kohut actually told me once that he thought "Ferenczi had the right idea." That meant that Kohut, like Ferenczi, believed that there was a good deal to be said for responding to a patient in whatever ways the patient experienced as therapeutic, even if these ways would not be endorsed by traditional psychoanalysis. It is thus not only interesting—but also fortunate for me—that Kohut did not practice, at least with me, in the way he subscribed to in theory. My experience of Kohut was that he skillfully followed the first step in his sequence for therapeutic action but that he did not adhere rigidly to his second step of confining himself to explanations; rather, he attempted to respond in whatever ways *he* could that might be healing for *me*. Kohut would usually listen quietly and receptively and respectfully, sometimes for a long time, before he spoke. What he actually said—and he offered many carefully considered observations and explanations—was usually of secondary importance, to me. I can barely recall any of it. But it did not matter. The way he related to me harmonized with what *I* needed at the time: acceptance and optimism, delivered with warmth and kindness.

As I have described on another occasion (Bacal, 2006), one of the most therapeutically salutary responses Kohut offered me was an encouraging arm around the shoulder at an especially dispiriting time when we were facing yet another 2-week break.[14] Yet, Kohut was evidently conflicted at times about offering responses that were at variance with his conception of psychoanalysis as a structured theory.

TOWARD A PROCESS THEORY OF THERAPEUTIC SPECIFICITY AND A FURTHER DEFINITION

When Kohut publicly defined interpretation as the only legitimate analytic response, he limited the scope of his first step in therapeutic cure, that of the *process* of empathic understanding. When the analyst listens in order to construct empathically informed, but theoretically organized explanations, or interpretations, his observational field and organization of the data so obtained, are necessarily shaped and constricted thereby. Interestingly, the more my work was guided by the expansion of Kohut's second step, explanation, in therapeutic cure—what I have called "optimal responsiveness"—the more I felt challenged to explore the first step, empathic understanding, because this step, in effect, constitutes a process of discovery of what the particularity of response might be that the patient may experience as therapeutic. That is, in recasting Kohut's second step in this way I was, in effect, deepening my understanding of Kohut's first step (empathic attunement)—with the recognition of the inherent specificity of the empathic method. I did not alter this first step as articulated: empathically informed understanding. But, with Carlton, I began, through specificity theory, to challenge what is meant by the *process* of understanding (Bacal & Carlton, 2008, 2010).

To reiterate: In expanding Kohut's second step from explanation to optimal responsiveness, I was not only asserting what was officially unrecognized, yet clinically evident—that the nature of therapeutic experience and therefore, possibilities for therapeutic responsiveness, are both much wider than generally acknowledged and simultaneously particular for that patient. I was also beginning to conceptualize its underlying *theory*—that of *the specificity of therapeutic process.*

Self psychologists who have critiqued optimal responsiveness as "not psychoanalysis" have based their critique on my broadening the nature of response in Kohut's second step for therapeutic cure while ostensibly downplaying the first step. Kohut's second step is that the analyst interprets to the patient what she has gleaned from the first step, empathic attentiveness. In effect, these criticisms focus inappropriately on the second step of this process as the definer of psychoanalysis. Rather, we propose that the two steps—understanding and response—not only overlap; they are inextricably linked, one with the other. We must now acknowledge that the measure of a therapy as psychoanalysis is neither "empathy" nor "response," but rather constitutes the fullness and complexity of both steps. In other words, the sine quo non of psychoanalytic therapy is not empathy culminated by verbal interpretation as the response in the second step, but the entire process that includes understanding the complex mental states of another, and discerning the needed therapeutic response that may or may not be possible within the ineluctably reciprocal process of that particular dyad—which may also be affected by the impact on it of adjacent and distant systems.

Psychoanalytic therapy comprises the quest to understand through *process* the inner life of another and to discern a useful response that may arise from that quest. In effect, specificity theory conceptualizes at the level of *understanding* understanding—that is, of *all* that goes into that process—and offers a new paradigm for therapeutic action. *Specificity theory states that our understanding is the product of each uniquely constituted dyad, comprising all of who each participant is, including the therapist's theories, and that optimal therapeutic responsiveness is comprehended by in-depth appreciation of the specificity of reciprocally emerging dyadic process, which determines therapeutic possibility for any particular dyad.* Through specificity theory, the limits to the usefulness of any formalized psychoanalytic structure theory on understanding, and of the therapeutic response that it entails, become more apparent.

A process theory that underscores specificity thereby also enjoins us to be aware that, however efficacious empathy or interpretation might be as therapeutic responses,[15] neither of them is the only response that is always experienced as therapeutically optimal, or even useful, by every patient. Specificity theory notifies us that neither is to be privileged in our work. Interpretive explication, however hallowed it may generally be regarded, is not the only response that constitutes therapeutic effect. Similarly for empathy, *the* response pre-eminently (albeit unofficially) regarded as therapeutic by self psychologists. Both kinds of responses may, at times, even be experienced adversely. Although I was not feeling the despair that Kohut's suicidal patient was suffering when he offered her his two fingers to hold (Kohut, 1981), had Kohut interpreted his sense of my need for an arm around my shoulder rather than offering it, at that time, I believe I would have experienced it as a somewhat hollow response. In my analysis with Kohut, I discovered that neither his explicit therapeutic action of offering empathic attunement or interpretation constituted the *only* ways that *I* experienced him being optimally responsive to my therapeutic needs. I have elaborated this more fully elsewhere (Bacal, 2006).

NOTES

1. Joseph Natterson (1991) gives extensive substance to this view in his book, *Beyond Countertransference.*

2. Since then, the ethos of the Department has shifted toward more "behaviorally-oriented" perspectives.

3. In my view, this was the essence of the heresy for which Alexander was marginalized by the psychoanalytic establishment. The concept of the corrective emotional experience has not only been maligned by traditional psychoanalysis, it has been remarkably misapprehended (see Bacal, 1990).

4. Stories abounded amongst the residents about the challenge posed in applying successfully for the coveted acceptance for training in a psychoanalytic institute, especially when facing the "many-headed monster" of assessors in Chicago, where most of our senior teachers had qualified.

5. My experience, during my first analysis, with Michael Balint, was similar. In later years, I became very interested in Balint's theory of primary love, which in retrospect also felt personally relevant, but Balint worked with me much as a classical analyst would do (see Bacal, 2006). Soon after Michael died, in 1970, I learned from Enid Balint that it had been many years since he had engaged in this kind of regressive analytic work with his patients (Enid Balint, personal communication, 1970).

6. No separate session was set aside for this supervision. The student, whose analysis is five times a week, talks about his case as part of his associations during these sessions. Undertaking this form of supervision was voluntary, and the candidate was required to complete an additional case under the traditional form of psychoanalytic supervision.

7. See Andre Haynal's (1989) informative and scholarly account of Michael Balint's and Sandor Ferenczi's contributions to psychoanalysis in *Controversies in Psychoanalytic Method: From Freud and Ferenczi to Michael Balint.*

8. Balint taught that, whenever you feel something when treating a patient, you should consider it as a possible symptom of the patient's illness.

9. Like Ferenczi, Balint experimented in the analytic setting with respect to potentially therapeutic responsiveness to patients in archaic states (Balint, 1968). Balint clearly admired Ferenczi, yet regarded his mentor as lacking sufficient discipline in his experimentation.

10. ". . . let it be understood that analytic technique requires of the physician that . . . the treatment must be carried out in abstinence. By this I do not mean physical abstinence alone . . . I shall state it as a fundamental principle that the patient's need and longing should be allowed to persist in her, in order that they may serve as forces impelling her to do work and make changes (Freud, 1915, p. 164).

11. Elliott Markson (personal communication) has referred to the importance of "being able to make a dent" in the analyst.

12. David Terman was at this time also implicitly offering a process perspective on treatment when he suggested the term, "dialogue of construction" to characterize it. "The dialogue is the structure . . ." (Terman, 1998, p. 74).

13. How this patient actually experienced what Kohut did, we cannot know, and analysts have, since that famous moment, debated whether he could have done

just as well by interpreting her need for human contact; or, some felt, perhaps she would have done even better had Kohut offered her his whole hand rather than just a couple of fingers.

14. I was seeing Kohut for 3 sessions every other week, traveling to Chicago from Toronto.

15. Kohut asserted that the idea of empathy should be applied only to the process of data gathering. However, as we (Bacal & Carlton, 2010) have argued, empathy may also be experienced as a response, which may—or sometimes may not—be felt as therapeutic.

6

The Foundational Perspectives of Specificity Theory

Therapeutic action informed by specificity theory derives from three foundational perspectives: (1) specificity theory focuses on therapeutic possibility; (2) therapeutic possibility is inextricably linked with optimal responsiveness; and (3) optimal responsiveness draws new attention to both the specificity and variability of therapeutic possibility and their dependence on the fit of each particular dyad.

SPECIFICITY THEORY FOCUSES ON THERAPEUTIC POSSIBILITY

For therapeutic effect, it is not only legitimate, but essential, that the therapist attempt to tailor the treatment to each patient. The therapeutic engagement must necessarily and continually be monitored and adjusted, as far as possible, to fit the specific and ever-changing needs, capacities, and limitations of both participants, regardless of what constitutes the therapist's structured psychoanalytic model. Therapist and patient must *find out* how they need to be, and what they need to do, together, to be therapeutic. Each encounter is most usefully approached as one where a potentially therapeutic couple has never been before. The overarching focus is the discovery or co-creation of reciprocal responsiveness that will optimally meet the particular patient's therapeutic needs. This specificity, as Carlton has described (see chapters 1 and 2), is based upon a consideration of psychoanalytic treatment at the *level* of *process*, which constitutes a new *order* of theory. Specificity theory thus conceptualizes at a different level of abstraction than more traditional psychoanalytic theories that conceptualize at the level of structure.

This way of conceptualizing psychoanalytic treatment and its application requires that the analyst continuously understand herself as she is affected, uniquely, through engagement with the particular patient, and to monitor the precipitates of her own history as they converge with those of her patient to determine their therapeutic potential as well as their limitations.[1] As demanding as this might be, commitment to doing the best we can with our patients requires that we ask no less of ourselves.

Spontaneous engagement, or "play" (see especially Parsons, 1999; Weinshel, 1998; Winnicott, 1971a, 1971b; Foehl, 2010; Ringstrom, 2001, 2010) can at times constitute the essence of effective psychotherapy, as it may emerge significantly within the specificity of process of the participants in a particular dyad. The early view of the Boston Group's Process of Change Study Group (Stern et al., 1998), which regarded the "something more than interpretation" to comprise therapeutic effect has since been modified (Stern et al., 1998; see chapter 9) to encompass a systems perspective in which no particular way to "be with" a patient is privileged. Foehl (2010) has recently presented a process perspective on play that is very much in accord with specificity theory. Foehl encourages us "to rethink anew our process without the encrustations of theory . . . [and to adopt] a critical "humorous" acceptance of multiple perspectives from the open ground of an epistemological pluralism." We think Foehl might like our "rabbi" story in chapter 2.

The following vignette visibly entails "play" as important; it also illustrates how patient and therapist found playfulness as a way of being together in a new, significantly specific way, in their process.

Stephen and I were working on a familiar theme—how depressively and desperately he is caught up with authority, with the one who "knows" what he should do. We understand that he appears compelled both to defy and comply (e.g., by delaying to do something that feels expected or working endlessly to get it just right) with the result that it takes him an inordinately long time to complete anything—or sometimes even to discover what makes sense for him to do. Understanding afforded by Classical structure theory, as well as by concepts of self psychology and pathological accommodation (Kohut, 1977; Brandchaft, 2004, 2007) have emerged as relevant in reflectively "working through" this problem over time. Stephen fights against internally organized burdensome demands for perfection while simultaneously seeking to meet them—both of which constitute reactions to precipitates of his relationship with his father.

I have felt that, in some ways, Stephen and I have struggled similarly in our relationship, and we have talked about this. Earlier in the analysis, I had on occasion, felt expectant tension about whether I would come through with just what Stephen needed from me; at times, he used to insist that I should give him "the answer" which, he implied, I undoubtedly knew, but withheld. We had understood this as both the expression of a desperate fantasy that if he could access his father's (my) omniscience he would then be "truly" smart. At times, we could also apprehend it as the expression within an "idealizing transference" of a developmental need to experience a different kind of father responding with useful fatherly advice. At other times, I experienced as slightly jarring Stephen's need seemingly to demonstrate his superior intellectual knowledge. Toward the end of this session, I felt there was more a sense of working together—or rather, a quality of playing with some of these, now familiar, themes.

At the start of the following session, Stephen brought out a deck of cards, and asked me to pick one—in my mind. He then took the cards away, and produced cards again. "Is your card there?" "No," I acknowledged, openly impressed. "It is not there." Then, with friendly, generous flair, Stephen showed me how the trick was done. The cards were all face cards, but they were all different, in both lots, so of course, "my card" would not be there.

I had been so focused on the possibility of his "knowing" in this magical way what was in my mind that, for a time, I was entertaining the possibility that he could actually do this. I slowly began to realize that we were, now, in our process, experiencing quite specifically a creatively transformed version of how Stephen and his father had related in a pathological way, even a "crazy" way (Stephen's description). We now found ourselves playing (literally and figuratively), with my allowing—and enjoying—him as really knowing, but with neither one of us having actually to be omniscient, or depreciated, i.e., made to feel stupid, or inadequate. Indeed, I felt immensely entertained by Stephen, and I believe he felt this in my responsiveness. And he was looking forward to hearing how the trick would go over when I showed it to my family members later.

During the session, and then later on when I shared with Stephen what I had written, we did some "analysis" of what had happened between us. I acknowledged that I was in some ways a bit like him. For a moment, I had been unable to think about how he might have done this (other than by reading my mind), because I was inclined to attribute omniscience to an admired other who seemed to offer this as a condition of relationship. As a child, my relationship with my mother was in certain respects similar to the one he experienced with his father. Like Stephen with his father, I had experienced myself with my mother as quite smart. While not being "perfect" for her was not an option, it was also clear that she was indisputably "the" smart one.

I also told Stephen that in another respect, too, I had felt in his presence a little like how he must have felt with his father. I spoke of my irritation at times when he would demonstrate his cleverness but that I had never addressed it because it was always subtle, fleeting, and lighthearted. Stephen told me that this was how his father actually behaved. "If only he had spoken in an openly depreciating way, it might have been easier." I then realized something that I had not understood until now. I had been taught to experience my mother's brilliance specifically in the way that Stephen had learned to accept his father's—through her sweet, subtle, yet unquestionably superior attitude. Now, though, Stephen's "offering" his "omniscience" by implying that he would "know" the card I was thinking of, i.e., could read my mind, was also an offer of something that felt new, and therapeutic: engaging the specificity of a shared problem—the unquestioning idealization of a "superior" mind—in a different way—a way that enabled us both to look only "magically" omniscient, but really clever.

As Stephen was leaving the session, he offered a grammatical critique of one of the words in my write-up of the vignette. I thanked him—I was truly grateful for this—and I did not feel a trace of annoyance.

THERAPEUTIC POSSIBILITY IS INEXTRICABLY LINKED WITH OPTIMAL RESPONSIVENESS

In addition to the analyst's sustained empathic attentiveness to her patient's and her own subjective states, therapeutic possibility depends upon whether the analyst can respond optimally to these needs. Within specificity theory, the field of analytic observation is expanded to include discernment of the response that the analysand expects from his analyst, because when the expression of a psychological need occurs in the patient, whatever follows may be experienced by the patient as a response to that need. That is, therapeutic effect is dependent upon both the continuous operation of the analyst's sustained empathic attentiveness to her patient's and her own subjective states, and the analyst's response to a patient's expectation that his particular therapeutic needs are going to be met. Optimal responsiveness and, therefore, therapeutic effect may usefully emerge from the influence of a variety of structured psychoanalytic theories that may contribute to the *possible* understandings of the interactions within a particular analytic dyad at any given point in time.

Specificity theory itself is not a theory that posits defined stages of development, universal mental structures, or innate motives (such as drives, or even relatedness), or defined disorders or prescribed ways of being with patients. Structured theories, such as classical psychoanalysis, ego psychology, object relations theory, Kleinian theory, and more "traditional" self psychology, conceptualize the mind as a self-contained entity that can be objectively observed, relatively independent of the influence of the observer, and understood through universally applicable principles and changed through prescribed techniques. Structured theories offer us rich and complex descriptions of possible states of organization between analyst and analysand. Specificity theory holds that such theories must be used intelligently, as they are only one possible organization of process and then perhaps applicable only for a point in time.

Therapeutic effect as inextricably linked with optimal responsiveness therefore privileges the influence of experiential awareness that emerges unpredictably via the specific interaction between analyst and analysand. This awareness may or may not reflect the elements of any recognized structured theory. It may also entail the application of other "theories" or models that the two participants bring from a myriad of other sources whether or not consciously held or formally articulated.

In contrast to the traditional psychoanalytic view that verbal interpretation of certain kinds is both the only mutative response as well as the only correct mode of intervention, the analyst's responsiveness properly and effectively draws upon a rich palette of both the verbal and the nonverbal in order to promote optimal therapeutic effect. All of this implicitly contradicts the notion that there can ever be one universally applicable analytic approach.

OPTIMAL RESPONSIVENESS DRAWS NEW ATTENTION TO BOTH THE SPECIFICITY AND VARIABILITY OF THERAPEUTIC POSSIBILITY AND ITS DEPENDENCE ON THE FIT OF EACH PARTICULAR DYAD

Therapeutic effect is centrally associated with the therapeutic fit between the two participants—between that analysand's therapeutic needs and that analyst's capacity to respond to them. Despite apparently striking differences, there may be remarkably harmonious fits in which there is safety and affection. And, despite apparently striking similarity, it is sometimes very hard to find a good fit. But, the spectrum of fit or misfit is not a static event, and may alter unpredictably and sometimes quite surprisingly over time. Therapeutic effect is specific to each analytic pair, in effect, to the potential and the limitations of the particular analytic dyad within which each participant responds to each other in the moment and over time. The nature of the fit, or linkage, is specific and variegated: of origin, culture, outlook, humor, values, development, therapeutic quest, motivation, trauma, or disruption, etc. that may emerge as significant within their process.

Limitations may comprise constraints of all sorts—professional and personal. And a dyadic system may be impacted by an adjacent or distant system, which can constrain the capacity of the dyad for optimal mutual responsiveness. Here are a few very brief illustrative situations, whose specificity variously derives from the analyst's professional training; who the analyst "is," and her limits, within different contexts; and from the pressure of an adjacent system.

In her analysis, the analysand, herself an analyst, pleaded with her analyst over months to please refer to her by her first name, not her professional name, Dr. X. He continued to use her professional name, Dr. X. As her frustration, disappointment, and anger mounted in the face of his refusal to meet her felt need for more warmth and personal recognition that use of her first name represented to her, the analyst finally said to her, "I cannot do it. My professional training proscribes such familiarity. I would violate my own standards of acceptable analytic behavior."

In a second example, an analytic student seeking additional clinical training in one of my study groups conveyed that, while she was aware of the value of staying with the validity of her patient's subjectivity, she was also becoming aware that something within herself—in effect, the sense of conviction attending her own subjectivity—at times tended to interfere with her doing so. She gave as an example the distress of one of her patients when the phone rang in session, even though she would not pick up the call. This, he told her, really upset him, and he didn't know why the analyst would allow this to go on. He was quite adamant that it took her attention away from him, and that it significantly disrupted the work they were doing. She, however, not only did not share these views, she also found it really difficult to take his distress seriously. After all, she told me, it was only the telephone ringing! She was struck by how differently she felt in a situation where she had no difficulty "staying with" a patient's painful experience that whenever his wife was on the phone, it was evidence that she was betraying him sexually with other men. She could respond to his experience by conveying that she could appreciate how this must torment him.

In response to my query about how she might explain how differently she felt about these two situations, she told me that what helped her to respond in the way she did to the patient whose wife was on the phone was that, in contrast to the other patient, this one seemed able at times to hold to some small possibility that what he was otherwise convinced of might not always be so; and therefore she could anticipate the possibility of her responsiveness relieving the intensity of his pain over time, if not relieving him of his delusion. A striking example of how the potential for empathic understanding and optimal therapeutic responsiveness can differ with the therapist's experience about a particular capacity, or not, in the patient, which apparently reflected what she herself struggled with, specifically, in process. In effect, this therapist was different in each situation. Although our understanding could benefit from much more information about the therapist, we might consider that her initial request for help with regard to a problem attending her feeling stuck in the validity of the rightness of her own subjectivity, or perspective, merits particular attention. Whether this work would most usefully be carried out at the level of therapy—which, we suspect, most analysts would likely assert—or addressed in the context of particular dyadic situations in supervision, is a question that we consider extensively in chapter 10.

Here are two brief examples of how an adjacent system can affect the specificity of optimal therapeutic responsiveness.

A therapist told her supervisor that after she and her patient met after the Christmas Holiday break, she wished she had told her patient that she could contact her during the break if she wished to do so. There had been no crisis—just the therapist reflecting that, in effect, it might have been better for the purpose of maintaining a thin relational link with this somewhat relationally distant patient who seemed to have started to come a little closer recently. The supervisor asked the therapist what made her not say that to her patient. She thought for awhile and then said, "Well, I have two small children . . ."

An analyst had been working successfully with a woman with a significant traumatic history. She needed frequent contact in the evenings for support with flashbacks that were stimulated through their work together. The analyst understood the patient's need, felt that such response was therapeutic, and had no difficulty extending it. However, at one point in the treatment, the analyst's husband sustained a fairly serious neck injury. He could no longer tolerate his wife spending evening time with this patient. He required his wife's quiet and consistent presence through the recovery process. This limitation from an adjacent system then limited the analyst's capacity to respond to her patient's need for evening call.

Therapeutic possibility available to any particular therapeutic dyad (or to the members of any therapeutic constellation, such as a couple, a group, or a family) develops at the interface between a particular therapist's and a particular patient's capacities and constraints to respond to each other from moment to moment and over time in specific emerging context. Therapeutic fit and thereby therapeutic possibility are variously affected by the therapist's experience of reciprocal responsiveness from the patient in particular ways. This constitutes dimensions of interaction that transcend the narrow perspective of the concepts of transference and countertransference (a topic we address in some detail in chapter 8).

Therapeutic fit is significantly related to the therapist's commitment both to stretch herself to meet the patient's therapeutic needs as well as to recognize the limitations that would strain her capacity to respond effectively. Therapeutic fit available to a particular dyad will become evident in the responses of the participants to one another and only knowable after the fact. The nature of therapeutic fit that determines therapeutic possibility is both much wider than generally acknowledged, and simultaneously more specific—to the particular participants. This is preeminently depicted in the following example.

Karen, Wheeler, and Dr. B

This clinical illustration may strike you as a tad surprising if your appreciation of the remarkable emotional responsiveness of the minds of dogs—at least some dogs—does not quite approach mine. I have always kept my dog with me in my consulting room, unless a patient objects (I inquire about this before the first consultation). When I first began to do this, many years ago, my (in part) classical background helped me rationalize this on the basis that Freud did too. As far as I'm aware, though, Freud's Chow was never his "associate."[2] Wheeler—whose nick-name is "We-dog"—*is*[3] mine, and he plays a variably important part in the therapy of my patients. For some, very little. For others, though, his presence is not insignificant. For Karen, it played a crucial—and specific—role. And the ways in which Karen experienced Wheeler's responsiveness as therapeutic are part of a weave of specificities of all three of us as they emerged in our process. Here is the backdrop to those specificities.

Wheeler is a 10-year-old English shepherd who joined me in my life when he was 16 months old.

There has almost always been a dog in my life. All of them except Wheeler were puppies when they came to live in our home. One of them had been especially important to me as a child when I sought a safe, reliable, and loving intimacy in refuge from my experiences of verbal abuse and emotional abandonment, by my mother.

I was looking for an English shepherd a few months after our golden retriever died at age 13. I found Wheeler in Oregon through the English shepherd rescue service. Dog person that I am, I flew from my home in Los Angeles to Portland, from where I drove 60 miles north to the little town of Dallas to meet Wheeler. Wheeler's owner recognized early on that her absence throughout the day was making Wheeler very lonely, and she transferred him to "foster care," where he had been living for about a year with two kind ladies. Although Wheeler and I only had a brief meeting, we seemed to connect well, and I made arrangements with his foster parents to adopt him and he was flown to us in Los Angeles a couple of months later.

For some time after he arrived, Wheeler was skittish and apprehensive. Everything that was unfamiliar to him—and there was much of this—seemed to upset and frighten him. It took him six months before he calmed down, and it would take him more than a year before he would play in any way at all. We do not think he had been physically abused, but it was not unlikely that he had been traumatized by his experience of separation (two, now) from people to whom he had become somewhat attached. Despite his agitation, Wheeler bonded to me almost immediately, and very strongly—and likewise I to him.

Wheeler is friendly and affectionate to others who are comfortable with him and who like him, but he tends to be somewhat uninterested in those who are indifferent to him—probably a bit like his Dad. Wheeler follows me wherever I go, and stays with me, all the time, in his "forever" home, of which he is very protective.

English Shepherds are working dogs, "farm collies," especially known for their protectiveness and for their attuned attentiveness to the farmer's wishes. Perhaps this is why Wheeler regards his primary job as being with me and helping me do my particular work; he has, surprisingly, turned out to be a remarkable sort of "therapy dog," working with me in my home office throughout the day.

I have wondered what may be in his mind as he greets someone with me at the door, and whether he wonders what their presence will be like today. There is evidence that he knows my (fairly consistent) daily schedule in the way he differentially anticipates the arrival of particular patients; and I suspect he has quite different feelings as he anticipates the arrival of particular patients, again, a bit like his Dad. Wheeler's level of arousal is particular to each person, his interest in everyone is different, and his way of relating to each is unique. He spends varying lengths of time with each patient, from a few seconds up to perhaps 10 minutes (not necessarily the same duration of time in each instance), and he exhibits a wide spectrum of doggie contact and quality with each—from a brief sniff, to a prolonged cuddle and scratch. He then walks back to his little rug in the far corner of the office behind my desk chair where he lies quietly, usually for the remainder of the session. I have not trained him nor even suggested to him that he do any of this. He has just always done this.

Someone who overtly gives him attention is not necessarily the one to whom he may respond. It seems to me—though this may reflect one of my several attributions to Wheeler—that he is particularly inclined to respond to those who he senses need him to be with them. I am a bit like that, so perhaps Wheeler, my sensitive farm collie, is responding as he thinks I might want him to. On one occasion, he got up from his rug in the middle of a session, and lay down at the feet of a patient who, until that moment, had kept his feelings of aloneness and fear of abandonment deeply hidden—certainly from me and probably from himself—but apparently not from Wheeler. The man started to reach down to touch Wheeler, then hesitated, and pulled his hand back. I asked why he stopped, and he replied, "I'm afraid that if I touch him, he will go away." Wheeler stayed with him for the rest of the session.

Without having words, without being able to hold an explicit idea of past and future, and unable to reflect on the meaning of behaviors for himself or the other, Wheeler may yet be making responsive, sustainable, and specific connection with various patients, in ways that for some are healing, or even essential, in order that they might connect with any intimacy to another at all. The latter was especially true for Karen.

Karen is a 45-year-old single woman from an upper class country family in southern England. She was abused, quite severely, both physically and emotionally, as a small child. She was frequently abandoned by her parents for weeks at a time, left with household staff or farmed out to neighbors when they were away. Karen was also repeatedly assaulted sexually by both her parents, and molested by almost every male member of the household staff, as well as by an acquaintance of her father, which he arranged. Apart from one of the live-in domestics, who would at times protect her by keeping her in her room at night, her refuge from this recurring trauma, and appalling betrayal, was the companionship of her dogs with whom she developed close bonds and with whom she spent as much time as possible.

Although Karen's experience of abuse far exceeded mine, she too found succor from her suffering by establishing close mutually caring connections with her dog friends in her adult life as well as in her childhood. While Karen has a number of human friends, and has had some loving relationships with men over the years, she has always lived alone, except for her dogs, whom she cares for as would a thoughtful and devoted mother to her children.

Karen's mother died when she was 11, and her father married a woman who had no interest in her. Karen had been in treatment since she was a teenager, which included periods of hospitalization for severe post-traumatic stress and occasional psychotic episodes. Karen's experience of therapy had largely been good. She especially valued her treatment with a particular psychoanalyst whom she came to trust and to become able to share painful, shame-filled feelings about her horrendously abusive experiences. However, several years into the treatment, he developed a brain tumor, and became intermittently psychotic. Tragically, he began to talk to Karen in sexually explicit ways that recalled and reactivated those early traumatic experiences, now in relation to him. Karen felt horribly betrayed, yet was unable to leave him; and then, within a year, he died. Karen worked with another analyst for a few years prior to seeing me. For some time, she gained valuable insights from that analyst; then she asked him for a referral to someone who could provide more of a "presence."

I saw Karen for appointments four times weekly, at somewhat different times. Wheeler soon knew what these times were, and eagerly anticipated Karen's arrival. When Karen would appear at the door of my office, she might greet me—in either a friendly or neutral sort of way—but mostly she would greet

Wheeler, with warm and happy tones. Wheeler responds by matching her affectionate greeting with wagging tail and burrowing nose and stays with her, allowing her to caress his fur and scratch his back (not something he readily does with anyone but me). This might continue for up to several minutes. Karen then sits down and Wheeler quietly walks back to his rug behind my desk. Karen and I then "start" our session—the most important part of which, though, has already happened.

I understood that Wheeler is the me that Karen would have wished to be able to trust and connect with like she can with Wheeler, yet my attempts to interpret her behavior with Wheeler as representing an "enactment" of the more deeply desired but fear-filled connection with me—one of the untrustable humans—has no effect. Karen does not refute these interpretations; she tacitly asserts their therapeutic irrelevance by simply not responding to them. While Karen does seems to value my presence and we do at times talk about problems of trust in our relationship, I have the strong impression that this would not be possible were it not for the presence of my associate therapist.

The therapeutic linkage that developed between Karen and Wheeler could be intelligibly conceptualized by the tenets of a number of formal psychoanalytic theories, such as attachment theory, self psychology, and object relations theory. Yet, it is important also to apprehend it at a higher level of abstraction and to consider the relevance of the specificity of healing in this relationship with Wheeler to psychoanalytic practice in general. Specificity theory gives substance to the value of Wheeler's responsivity to Karen through its recognition of the specificity of therapeutic responsiveness in the present other than verbal interpretations that link past experience with current behavior. From this perspective, therapists can be made more aware of the possibility of healing through their attuned presence, supporting their courage to "not know" just what will emerge as therapeutic. Wheeler preeminently sits in a position of not knowing, as the kinds of cognitive capacities that we, as humans, engage to "know" and to "analyze" are not available to him.

Karen started to assert herself with other people in ways that she had never done before in order to get the kind of help, and caring, that she has needed to counterbalance the devastating effects of the traumata she sustained during her childhood. The therapeutic yield from the connection between Wheeler and Karen—indeed, between the three of us—was crucially specific to our own histories and to our own sensibilities and sensitivities as they emerged in our process, where we discovered what our particular capacities were to be therapeutic together.

In the next chapter, we will look more closely at the clinical consequences of the shift from the universality of structure to the specificity of process.

NOTES

1. We believe Wachtel (1986, p. 60), in part, implied such a view when he stated, "It is essential that the analyst address the unique individuality of the patient" . . . [and] "We are always observing something that occurs in relation to us, and not just to us as screens or phantoms, but to us as specific flesh and blood human beings sitting in the consulting room."

2. Yet, there is the story of how one of Freud's Chows, so sensitive to his moods, responded to his pleasure that his patient, Abram Kardiner, indicated being deeply understood by an interpretation, suddenly leaped onto Kardiner's chest and began licking his cheek (Craig Powell, personal communication, 2009).

3. Sadly, Wheeler died in August 2009, a little over a year before this book was published. But he was very much here when I wrote this vignette, so I am writing it as if he still is. His presence is still very much with me.

7

Clinical Consequences of the Shift from the Universality of Structure to the Specificity of Process

The primary consequence of a process view of mind versus a structure view of mind constitutes a *radical shift in epistemology*. This is a formal way of saying that a process view of mind changes the *how*, and *what* we, as psychoanalysts, know, in working with a patient. Specificity theory thus constitutes a new way of understanding psychoanalytic, or psychodynamic,[1] psychotherapy as process. While its perspectives are consistent with many aspects of other process theories, such as intersubjective systems theory, nonlinear dynamic systems theory, and complexity theory, as well as with other relationally-oriented intersubjective theories, as we described in chapter 1, it has a different focus: the co-creative discovery of what may, or may not, be therapeutically effective for the particular patient, given the specific capacities and limitations of the particular participants that emerge at that time, and over time.

When specificity becomes central in our consideration of process, the epistemological shift pre-eminently illuminates how the *who* of the participants in the particularity of their process will determine therapeutic effect. In other words, *these shifts in epistemology have significant clinical consequences*.

Specificity theory alters the very nature of therapeutic practice in three basic ways: (1) the role that formal psychoanalytic theory assumes in the therapeutic process; (2) the nature of the therapeutic response and the process through which the particular response is derived; and (3) the nature of the relationship between the patient and the therapist.

ALTERATION OF THE ROLE THAT FORMAL PSYCHOANALYTIC THEORY ASSUMES IN THE THERAPEUTIC PROCESS

In contrast to a theory of process, a structure theory serves a more explicit explanatory and guiding function within the treatment. Much of what the therapist knows about the patient and therapy is derived explicitly from the theory itself, even when the therapist assiduously attempts to apply its understanding individually. Structure theories, such as ego-psychology, object relations, Klein, Lacan, and self psychology offer the psychoanalytic therapist systematically formulated postulates to guide the understanding of the patient and the response to the patient. The theory itself offers the therapist knowledge of the patient's primary motivations, development, and the prescribed manner in which to helpfully intervene.

Within any given structure theory, psychoanalytic technique is premised upon and determined by the generalities which the theory conceptualizes. These generalities are based upon universal assumptions about man, his development and illness, and they give rise to established prescriptions by which to cure the patient of defined ills. For example, if man is believed to be motivated by unconscious drives and made ill by failure to renounce the gratification of infantile strivings—the Weltanschauung of traditional psychoanalytic theory—then it would be critical to refrain from gratifying any relational desires that the patient has of the therapist as this would interfere with the ways in which psychoanalytic technique is applied to make the unconscious determinants of those desires conscious. If man is believed to be motivated by a need to assure, or to restore, self cohesion, and to realize his ambitions and meet his ideals—the outlook of self psychology—the therapist must respond in prescribed ways that are consonant with these purposes. Specificity theory, on the other hand, recognizes that the constituents of formal theories comprise only some of the many ideas that we utilize to organize, understand and respond to, our patients.[2]

While we contrast specificity theory as a theory that embraces uniqueness and emergent order with structure theory as referring to a variety of theoretical systems that are relatively highly structured, specificity theory by no means dispenses with useful hypotheses, insights, and responses that emanate from structure theories. We recognize that such theory is critical to our work; we cannot think without it. But its role within the application of specificity theory is recast as providing possibilities, models to play with and argue against, not as a source of knowledge of any single patient. We therefore view psychoanalytic structure theories as hypotheses that must be consciously considered as such. The assumptions that underlie a structure theory must be identified and considered as to whether they are applicable to a particular patient at a particular moment in the therapy.

When the specificity of process is at the center of our consideration, the generalities intrinsic to the formalized concepts of structure theories can emerge as illustrative of a particular patient or of a therapist's specific relationship with a particular patient. Specificity theory can thus assist the therapist to think about and utilize more thoughtfully and intelligently the panoply of these theories that now abound to guide psychotherapy as generalities, in order to illuminate and think about any particular clinical moment. Structure theories of psychotherapy become simply another attribute among many that may influence a particular therapist about how to understand and be with his patient.

Unformulated Theory, Blinking, and the Dark Matter of Our Minds

In addition to formal psychoanalytic theory, with specificity theory we also attend to a plethora of other "theories," or "models," both conscious and unconscious, that may centrally influence the therapist's responsiveness to his patient. It is not so easy to discern the vast body of unformulated concepts that every analyst also ineluctably draws upon in understanding and responding to her patient. Specificity theory explicitly draws the therapist's attention to this type of theory and notes that it warrants our serious attention. Such theory derives from the diverse experience of the particular personal and professional life of the analyst, both past and present, and consciously and unconsciously, as well as from the Weltanschauung to which these give rise. Conceptually, this extends well beyond the narrow confines of *countertransference*, whether the latter is defined classically as impediment, or as consisting of all the analysts feelings[3] or organizing principles. Unformulated theory, like formal psychoanalytic theories, constitutes an aspect of who the analyst is, at any moment. It will inescapably play a part in determining the responses of the therapist toward her patient, and its therapeutic influence can be pivotal and profound. It may be implicitly and/or explicitly operative. However, its effect can be discovered only if we are aware that it exists.

In his book, *Blink*, New Yorker Science writer, Malcolm Gladwell (1995) has analyzed a vast number of psychological studies that demonstrate that the human mind develops many theories about its world through experiences and observations, many of which are never consciously held nor verbally articulated (25). The human mind continually unconsciously seeks out patterns in situations and behavior. These associations influence our thoughts, judgments, decisions and actions in a very rapid fashion (Gladwell, 50). Gladwell calls this "thin-slicing," the ability of our unconscious to find patterns in situations and behavior based on very narrow slices of experience (23). Not only do we premise many judgments on these unconscious theories, we are not aware that we are not aware (71).

According to Gladwell, "Thin-slicing is not an exotic gift. It is a central part of what it means to be human . . . We thin-slice because we have to, and we come to rely on that ability because there are lots of hidden situations where careful attention to the details of a very thin slice, even for no more than a second or two, can tell us an awful lot" (43–44).[4] Yet, this knowledge is based on a lifetime accumulation of unconscious theories about our world. Specificity theory explicitly notices the operation of thin-slicing, as one type among other types of informal theories to encourage the therapist to explore and examine continually the underpinnings of his judgments, bearing in mind Gladwell's admonition that most of us feel ignorant of the operation of these unconscious theories upon our reasoning even when provided with scientific evidence that they are influencing us (71).

The ubiquity and abundance of informal theory, conscious and unconscious, that influences who we are and how we behave may be analogous to the "dark matter" of the cosmos that lies between the stars which may constitute much more of space/time than the stars themselves.[5] Like the dark matter of space/time, unformulated "theory" does not easily lend itself to identification or description, yet to ignore it may be to disregard much of what is also central within psychoanalytic treatment.

THE ALTERED NATURE OF THE THERAPEUTIC RESPONSE AND THE PROCESS THROUGH WHICH THE PARTICULAR RESPONSE IS DERIVED IS ALTERED

Theories that are premised upon a structured concept of mind offer definite therapeutic methods and techniques. Structure theories provide a type of blueprint for the desired outcome of therapy, which then gives rise to designated responses in order to obtain the desired outcome. The product delimits the process. Aristotle expressed this as the distinction between what he called techne and phronesis, or episteme (Aristotle, *Nicomachean Ethics*), each of which connotes a different relationship between the means and the ends. The technique required to produce an object is defined by the endproduct. The method required to understand and respond to a person is itself a part of the creative process. The more experienced a therapist becomes with technique, the more expert he/she becomes—in certain contexts. For example, a cognitive behavioral therapist has an established protocol of treatment comprised of designated exercises to be worked through in a predetermined sequence in a determinate number of sessions, and instruments that continually monitor the patient's progress relative to symptoms reported at the onset of treatment. A classical analyst's structure understanding of mind gives rise to abstinence, anonymity, and neutrality together with verbal interpretation as prescribed curative response.

What we all "know," but variously find it difficult to quite acknowledge, is that, in many contexts, we cannot know what will work therapeutically for our patient and ourselves at any particular time. What then becomes of technique when there is no known or agreed upon end point, when it is the very act of creation in and of itself that is the focus of the work? Specificity theory does not recognize any universal goal of the therapeutic encounter, but endorses Bion's admonition that "desires for results, 'cure' or even understanding must not be allowed to proliferate" (Bion, 1967, p. 273). "The only point of importance in any session is the unknown . . . in any session, evolution takes place. Out of the darkness and formlessness something evolves" (272). For Bion, therapeutic effect "[derives] from the emotional experience with a unique individual and not from generalized theories imperfectly 'remembered'" (273). He has wryly noted that if the analyst feels he has seen the patient before, he is treating the wrong patient (273).

Specificity theory entails sustaining and tolerating uncertainty. The psychotherapist must attend to the context, the emergent, the disorganized and the unknown. Specificity demands that structured theories be used intelligently. The therapist must be aware of the assumptions inherent in the particular theory, the context from which the theory emerged and the aspects of a relationship that are attended to or privileged and those that are relatively discarded.

With specificity theory, technique and know-how are supplanted by an increased capacity to tolerate the anxiety of not knowing the response (and whatever theoretical substrate may underlie it) that could emerge as therapeutically useful for the particular patient, and possible for the therapist who is treating him. Practice informed by specificity theory engages with the patient without prescriptive or proscriptive responses and without guidelines. Such a process requires a unique use of the therapist's self in the psychoanalytic encounter.[6] When we really grasp the uniqueness and specificity of each therapeutic encounter, and when we deeply appreciate that the mind is created through and by the relationship, we are continually engaged in the moment to determine each time the responsiveness that will optimally meet the particular patient's therapeutic needs. This does not envision an analyst who necessarily becomes more expert in psychoanalytic technique, but rather one who increasingly gains comfort with not knowing and with sensing the use of himself or herself, both consciously and unconsciously, in engaging his or her patient's therapeutic needs.

Yet, as we emphasized in setting out the foundational perspectives of specificity theory in the last chapter, it is essential that the therapist allow herself to fit her responsiveness to each patient (Bacal & Herzog, 2003). Apprehending the *nature of process and its specificity* gives substance to the legitimacy of this variability. Such variability expresses the uniqueness that is intrinsic to the treatment engaged by a particular dyad and which precludes a priori knowledge of how the patient might be responded to optimally. As we have noted, responses that may emerge as therapeutic, or not, may include—in addition to the classical quatrain of quiet listening, clarification, confrontation, and interpretation—a wide range of non-verbal behaviors, *inter alia,* expressions of the analyst's attitudes and feelings such as smiling, encouragement, laughter, admiration, praise, humor, surprise, advice, perplexity, frowning, anger, crying, touching, making extra-analytic contact, and receiving or even giving a gift. Responsiveness that the patient experiences as therapeutically optimal can be mediated either by careful conscious deliberation, or even quite unconsciously. It can also emerge apparently spontaneously, which Ringstrom (2001) and Kindler (2010) address in terms of the improvisational. At times, the analyst may offer long periods of receptive listening and contemplative, reflective analysis in determining a response; at other times the analyst may usefully respond in a much more immediate, emotional and spontaneous way. *Specificity theory holds that all potentially therapeutic responses in the treatment situation are legitimately utilizable—with the proviso that they not interfere with the therapist's professional functioning or exceed either the therapist's or the patient's personal tolerance.* The analyst who utilizes specificity theory increasingly gains comfort with not knowing and sensing the use of himself, both consciously and unconsciously, in his engagement with his patient's therapeutic needs.

Optimal therapeutic responsiveness may entail reciprocal acceptance by the analyst of the patient's response to the analyst in a myriad of comparable ways. The nature and extent of the analyst's useful participation in the offered response may vary widely as well. *Within the specificity of a particular process,* the analyst seeks to apprehend the patient's therapeutic need at a given moment, and he seeks to discern the patient's expectation of a response to that need. The field of observation is thus expanded to include that particular patient's anticipated response from his therapist to his particular therapeutic need at that time, which in turn affects the therapist's response. The therapist's understanding of the patient and his response to the patient are shaped by the analyst's quest to be aware of the likelihood that when the expression of a need state occurs, whatever follows may be experienced by the patient as a response to this. Response and response to the response continually influence each other as therapist and patient find out how they need to be together, and what they can do together, to be therapeutic. There is no designated end-state or inherent point of termination. The methods and responses are co-creatively discovered as the therapy unfolds. Lachmann offers an interesting analogue of this in his analysis of a slow-motion film of the complex interactively regulated system, the "empathic exchange," of boxers who may enter the anticipated behavioral stream of the other to unconsciously predict each other's behavior. Lachmann considers that the nature of such improvisation is analogous to what may transpire between "mother and infant, therapist and patient, teacher and student, supervisor and candidate" (Lachmann, 2008, pp. 64–65). Lachmann appears to be drawing attention to the unique yet in some ways "predictable" sequences that obtain for a particular dyad who come to "know" each other's moves or play, similar to what Tronick understands as "thickness" (see chapter 9). Lachmann adds, however, that while the two boxers need only predict each other's behavioral sequence, the co-creation of empathic responsiveness "requires this and more" (p. 65). (See also Lachmann, 2010.)

From the perspective of specificity theory, therapeutic effect constitutes a function of the capability for requisite reciprocal responsiveness that emerges within the particular process of the specific participants interacting within their system (e.g., the dyadic system of psychoanalytic therapy, or the multi-person system of a group, or family).

Once again, we emphasize that this constitutes a *process*, whose therapeutic value does not rest on an objective standard. Its assessment will never be knowable in any "objective" sense, unless one undertakes the sort of evaluation that "outcome research" offers (see chapter 1). Yet, we can find opportunities, within the system comprising the specificity of process itself, for optimal therapeutic responsiveness (Bacal & Herzog, 2003, 642). Much depends upon "therapeutic fit."

The Importance—and Indeterminacy—of Therapeutic Fit and the Range of Therapeutic Possibility

However much we might want to believe we have a valid sense of "knowing" whether there would be a therapeutic fit between us and our patient, and what sort of theory or technique would work best for her or him, specificity theory teaches us that we must forgo these prognosticating exercises. Important as it is, "therapeutic fit," in whatever shape or form it may emerge, is never reliably predictable. That therapist and that patient must discover the most therapeutic ways of being together. This requires that the therapist consider, from moment to moment, not only what may be "effective" therapeutic responsiveness with that patient, but also whether he is capable of providing it.

In other words, apart from the likelihood that we will not infrequently find out what is optimally responsive for our patient at any particular time through our discovery that we are not providing it, we cannot know in advance whether that person's therapeutic needs will be met by our capacity to respond to them. Or, indeed, whether a treatment will even get off the ground. Bion's dry response to my inquiring during our first supervision session what he thought of my undertaking the analysis of a particular patient who had applied to the London Clinic of Psycho-Analysis was, "A patient may take one look at you and never want to see you again" (Bion, personal communication, 1965). During my next 45 years of analytic practice, I have had occasion to recall Bion's wry caveat. Sometimes, though, this takes more than one look; and at times, a patient may never leave us, and may benefit greatly from therapy over a long period of time. While we may come to feel that a certain *range of therapeutic possibility* obtains with a particular patient,[7] we may also be surprised to discover in the moment or/and over time how our ability to interact therapeutically with that patient may transcend this.

Stretching, Limitations, and a Word about the "Third"

I have found that in situations when I feel that I am reaching the limits of my ability to work effectively with a particular patient, my capacity to offer needed responsiveness emerges as a function of my willingness, or felt ability, to stretch myself to meet my patient's therapeutic needs, along with my awareness that doing so will not excessively strain my ability to respond therapeutically. My patient may also need to discover her capacity, and her limits, too, for stretching, in order to work with me.

Whatever capacities we may discover for such stretching[8] may be variously affected, as we noted earlier (p. 65) by the impact of adjacent systems. We have wondered whether what some psychoanalysts refer to as the "third" constitutes one of these systems. Would the analyst's capacity to "stretch" herself be facilitated by its utilization?

Much has been written and discussed about the idea of the third; a 2006 IARPP colloquium was recently its theme, based on a paper by Lewis Aron (online colloquium, October 30—November 19, 2006; see also Aron, 2006). Of the many aspects, or varieties, of "third" that have been put forth (and there are now a plethora of them), the one that makes most sense to me, and that feels useful, is its characterization as a shared experience co-created by analyst and analysand that can be helpful in negotiating impasses in treatment (as emphasized by Pizer [1998], echoed by Aron [IARPP online colloquium November 14, 2006], and elaborated by Benjamin [2004]). Both Aron and Benjamin liken the third to the "potential space" of Winnicott (1971, pp. 107–110) where mother and baby somehow find a place and way to connect. According to Benjamin (2004), who vividly illustrates its function in cases where analyst and analysand are stuck in an often hurtful "doer and done-to" mode, the sense of third, if achievable, may constitute a space for cooperative endeavor.

I have wondered whether this theory of the third might have made sense of my effort (which I described in chapter 5) to transform a disruptive experience in my analysis with Balint into a therapeutic one. I had suggested to Balint—when he was hurling hurtful (and unusable) confrontations at me during the early days of the analysis, that he consider a metaphor for a different way of working—that we might be like two children sitting on the floor side by side, leaning against the couch looking at something together and discussing what each of us saw in it. Did this constitute a plea to him that we try to find a way, such as Benjamin describes, of "creating a dyadic system that contains by virtue of mutual reflection . . . [and thereby transforms our] conflict around responsibility into a shared third, an object of joint reflection" (Benjamin, 2004, p. 15)? This description of the "third" appears at first glance to offer a possible conceptualization of that situation. We would, in this way, have created a different therapeutic situation, characterized by a *specific experience* of sharing (see Herzog, 1998), rather than my being the object of judgmental confrontation. Yet, conceptualizing this as a shared "third" does not accord with my experience. I was desperately trying to elicit *from my analyst* a particular kind of responsiveness that would feel specifically therapeutic for me—that *we* share something interesting to both of us in a way that excluded oppressive inequality and judgment. I also sensed that he would have to stretch himself a whole lot in order to do this.

The notion of third may skirt the recognition of the incapacity of that analyst and analysand to transcend for therapeutic purpose the limits of their particular dyadic capacity. It is important to recognize when this may be the case. In such situations, the invocation of the theory of the third could constitute an attempt of the dyad to do an end run around their limitations. In contrast, when impasses are courageously engaged by both parties, as Jessica Benjamin illustrates with her case example (see Benjamin, 2004), the resulting struggle may embrace a remarkably therapeutic—though, at times, quite painful—experience through overt sharing of their specific limitations in context. The experience on the part of both analyst and analysand in situations such as these centrally relates to the question as to whether that analyst and that analysand can stretch themselves adequately in specifically important ways. We have described two instances that illustrate this: in chapter 6, the situation in which the analyst shared with his patient that his analytic credo precluded his calling her by her given name, which for her, precluded the intimacy with her analyst that she yearned for. This was also vividly depicted in the analysis of Beth with Lucyann Carlton (in chapter 3) where the patient desperately felt she needed the analyst actually to hold her, which Lucyann felt she could not do.

We wonder whether the conceptualization of third—unless specifically useful for a particular dyad, such as consultation—may constitute an unwarranted reification. The particular metaphor of the third comes from a mechanistic epistemological system incompatible with thinking when operating within a phenomenological epistemology, such as specificity theory. Within specificity theory, we might ask, what third? Everything brought into the room with two people is brought in with them and through them; there isn't any "thing" "outside" them, certainly not some isolated factor or belief to which they resort. Benjamin uses the idea of the third to create or to hold the possibility for the dyad that as the two interact there is a third way of being not envisioned by or within either one alone. Experience conceptualized in this way may actually constitute *specifically* unfolding therapeutic experience by analytic dyads in a variety of ways, through reflecting, playing, enacting, "self-disclosing" etc., when attempting to work through painful impasses to an equitable solution. The advantage of "third" is in supporting a concept of change. The disadvantage is the mechanistic, thereness-otherness of it, something out there from someplace else that can enter into the dyad in a unidirectional movement and not influenced by who each person is. This constitutes a lower order of conceptualization, from another realm of thought.

A valuable concretization of the idea of the *third* may, especially in situations of felt impasse or misfit, comprises consultation, or supervision. It is important, though, to keep in mind that this places the analytic dyad in a triadic system of interlacing specificity, which will have its own particular capacities and limitations (see chapter 10). Another evident and potentially useful concretization of the "third" is the modality of treatment that we call couples therapy.

The ability for mutual "stretching" can affect the "fit" of the dyad, and may significantly depend upon that analyst's and that analysand's ability to respond *in specific ways to each other*. The clinical consequence of this is that effective patient-therapist relationship turns out to be much more reciprocally responsive than psychoanalysts have been willing to acknowledge (see Bacal & Thomson, 1996, 1998).

The Specificity of Reciprocity

As we now explore therapeutic process more deeply through the lens of specificity theory, we are discovering that therapeutic process is ineluctably reciprocal, specifically. That is, reciprocally specific process may significantly affect the patient's therapeutic experience. It is not only the patient who brings conscious and unconscious expectations to his therapist. The analyst normally has a variety of conscious and unconscious expectations of the patient, many of which are responded to by the patient during therapy. While some of these expectations on the part of the therapist are ubiquitous—such as the patient arriving for sessions, talking sometimes, and tacitly or explicitly acknowledging the usefulness of what the therapist has to offer, as well as conveying this concretely by paying his bill—many more are specific to particular analyst-patient pairs. Many expectations of either party may remain below the radar of each until they are not met. And the analyst as well as patient may experience disruption in their relationship when their expectations are not met. (ibid.). The complexity and specificity of such expectations are not adequately apprehended by the terms, "transference" and "countertransference," a topic we look at more closely in chapter 8.

The analyst's experience of the patient's specific responsiveness can be as crucial for a therapeutic process as the patient's experience of that of the analyst. Recognition of the specificity of reciprocal relatedness and its mutual regulation in any particular dyad can be pivotal to the therapeutic effect of that dyad.

ALTERATION OF THE NATURE OF RELATIONSHIP BETWEEN THE PATIENT AND THERAPIST

In psychoanalysis, the concept, "relationship," is linked to many sorts of experiences, which have been variously apprehended as "part object," "whole object," "selfobject," or mutually experienced relationships with distinctly delineated others (see Bacal & Newman, 1990). In focusing on the specificity of therapeutic effect, "relationship" becomes one of its functions, the nature of which may be different in any particular instance. And even a priori identification of the "relational" or of the "intrapsychic" as central to therapeutic effect gives way, from the perspective of specificity theory, to a consideration of what emerges at any time as pre-eminently therapeutic within the particular dyad. Either, or variously, both—or perhaps something else that we do not "know" about (see p. 75)—might be centrally implicated in the therapeutic process of a particular dyad.[9]

A therapist who is guided by a particular structure theory gains knowledge about the patient as if he is entirely separate from the therapist. In addition, he tends to relate from a position of authority: the one who knows about the patient as informed by his particular structure theory. Both these aspects of relatedness change when therapeutic practice is informed by specificity theory. When a therapist fully realizes the unique and creative nature of therapeutic relatedness articulated by specificity theory, a relationship of a fundamentally different nature obtains between therapist and patient. Specificity theory recognizes that the therapist, who he or she is, in process with the particular patient, is integral to a therapeutic relationship.

The following example depicts the clinical consequences of the shift from the universality of structure to the specificity of process, a shift that basically entails the recognition that the patient cannot be known or related to in any "objective," or "general" sense. The example illustrates that the ways in which the therapist comes to understand, respond, and relate to, any particular patient is inextricably linked to that therapist's knowledge of himself and who he is with the particular patient.

Dr. C and Dr. B

Dr. C, an assistant professor of Sociology at the University of Toronto, sought analysis with me in the early 1980s after attending one of my clinical seminars on self psychology in the extension program of the Toronto Institute of Contemporary Psychoanalysis.[10] Dr. C and I had been working well together in analysis for about a year. We both felt we were effectively grappling with one of his main struggles—to feel more a sense of himself, to feel more centered. It seemed to me that Dr. C's progress could be usefully apprehended from the perspective of self psychology theory, namely, the progressive development of an idealizing selfobject relationship, along with experiences of selfobject mirroring. I liked and respected my analysand, and felt that he reciprocated these feelings. We seemed to be a good "fit" in this respect, as well as in some other ways, which I shall describe shortly, even though our backgrounds were somewhat different. Dr. C's was British/WASP to Vancouver; mine was Rumanian/Jewish to Montreal.

Dr. C had told me that he felt badly that he could not make his father feel better about himself following his recent retirement. He had been a talented set designer for a well-known Canadian movie company in Vancouver, but retired early because he was feeling unwell. Dr. C thought his father was depressed. During his career, Dr. C's father had always prioritized a high standard of artistic excellence but this had not translated into commercial benefit. Dr. C's mother, on the other hand, authoritatively espoused the ideal of financial success, and took every opportunity to point out the material achievements of her son's older brother as an example of someone who had made a sensible choice of business as a vocation. Dr. C was struggling with feelings of disappointment in his father, even while he admired his principles, and felt resentment toward his mother for not valuing who he was because his chosen profession would not enable him to make a great deal of money. Yet Dr. C was not quite able to dispossess himself of considerable shame in not following a career that his mother would have admired and valued.

Dr. C had been talking about his frustration and sadness that his father never reacted when he would do something "bad" as an adolescent. He described a particular incident in which he experienced especially strong disappointment in his father when he was arrested for dangerous driving. His father seemed not know what to make of it; he was silent, and just appeared sad. There seemed no way to talk about it and they never did—and this was the case in so many instances. Dr. C felt still felt confused about this, and cried as he remembered his father's silence.

We could analyze a good deal of the complexity of his feelings, much of which, it seemed to me, had to do with his not being able to bump up against a strong, idealizable father, with both of us contributing richly to its working through. In one session, I said that I now could see more clearly why he has felt able to open up so freely to me. In addition to his feeling that I was "trustworthy," he must value the very way we were interacting in analysis; it was so important to him to feel free to talk openly about what troubled him—what he felt he could never do in relation to either of his parents—in particular, sharing his feelings of disappointment, anger, and shame. He left the session with a spontaneous expression of gratitude. I was feeling good about how we were together and what we were doing together. Some of this, however, was soon to change, as the specificities of our process unfolded.

Dr. C was somewhat familiar with psychoanalytic theory, and had alluded from time to time about studying it formally, but he was uneasy about doing this because he felt he might be motivated by an inclination to accommodate to my wish that he do so. I realized that he was picking up some of my subjectivity. I was interested in his interest in this, and we had talked about what it would entail. I thought he would enjoy and benefit from the training, but as far as I was consciously aware, I felt no "need" for him to do this. It seemed to me that he had been moving in that direction himself, and I was responding positively. At one point, Dr C conveyed his interest in actually applying for psychoanalytic training. He had recently attended two major psychoanalytic conferences held in Canada in 1987—the 35th International Psychoanalytic Association Congress and the Canadian Psychoanalytic Society's annual meeting. Though he railed against the conservative and rigid theoretical perspectives that he thought were too pervasive at both, he remained interested in, and valued, psychoanalytic thinking. Soon after attending these conferences, he decided that he wanted to undertake the training. He told me that, with this decision, he felt truly like himself for the very first time.

Yet, it was also not surprising to me that his actually going forward with this would hinge upon a number of problematic considerations. The one I will highlight here is how Dr. C experienced me and what *I* had to offer *him* in continuing as his analyst. In the session after he shared his interest in pursuing training and implied that I might be his "training analyst," he expressed a reservation that reflected a concern about me that paralleled his concern about himself. He was worried that I might be too accommodating. I interpreted that he was worried that I would be like his father who had seriously disappointed him, as he never presented a stance of disciplined authority. He agreed, and reminded me that he was also concerned about his own tendency to overly accommodate, which manifested in various areas. If I am like that, he said, then he would be in considerable trouble (in continuing his analysis with me) since, because of his inclination to accommodate, he could never, in effect, truly find himself—his true sense of himself—with me. (Self psychologists may recognize the operation not only of Dr. C's anticipation of a failed idealizing selfobject relationship, but possibly also the anticipation of a certain kind of needed, but unavailable, twinship relationship with me.)

His evidence for my possibly being a wuss, as he termed it, was that I might be someone who needed gratitude. He referred to a case of mine that I had presented where I discovered that, in a particular context, I felt the need for gratitude from a particular patient who rarely expressed it. He told me about a session he had recently attended at the International Psychoanalytic Association meeting, where a particular analyst and his work were acclaimed. The analyst was in a wheelchair, having suffered a spinal injury some months ago. To Dr. C, his being there despite being confined to a wheelchair, as well as his demeanor, seemed to reflect that he "did not have any needs"—in particular, for recognition or flattery, or for any falling in with his views. As he talked more about this, he conveyed that that his (avowed) idealization of this analyst as someone who "had no needs" centrally ensured that he did not need to accommodate to anyone. He could, Dr. C conveyed, constitute his own authority. Being with such a person would enable him to deal effectively with the bewilderment attending his search for a deep sense of his own self, which determined a pervasive sense of uncertainty. He referred to other aspects of my responsiveness to analysands that he had read about. He valued my theory that supported an approach of keeping an open mind, of interacting with patients in the search for responsiveness that was therapeutically optimal. Yet, he conveyed that it was important to him that I not "provide." If I did, I was an accommodating wuss, who required gratitude. It was, rather, important to him that I maintain the "frame," that I "knew" what was right. Otherwise, I would be too much like his father, who never had a solid opinion, who would not confront anyone. If I were like that, perhaps I would not be the kind of mentor he needed, in effect, the kind of teacher he wished to emulate. This might also evoke his inclination to accommodate, thereby depriving him of the possibility of finding himself, and his true values, professionally as well as personally.

His major question at this juncture was, should he apply to the local contemporary institute or to the local traditional institute for analytic training? Dr. C talked with several friends and colleagues about this, and spoke with analysts at both institutes. He told me he was feeling drawn more to the structured curriculum at the traditional institute, where Freudian and historical perspectives were accorded more recognition. But which institute did I think he should apply to? It was important to him that I give him my opinion about which Institute would be best for him. He knew that I was a member of both training institutes, but I believe he sensed that my primary sense of affiliation was with the contemporary institute.

I responded by saying that I, too, leaned toward the more traditional institute as the one that would likely be the better choice for him. My response seemed to feel right to him; and that choice, he said, would ideally be served by my becoming his training analyst. And then, we faced another issue that was to affect whether Dr. C and I could continue with his analysis.

As I was a "training analyst" at both institutes, his choice would present no problem in this regard. However, financial considerations did. Dr. C asked me if I would reduce my fee further when he began the training. When we had begun to work together, I had already reduced it to a level that was well below my usual fee in order to accommodate his family budget. I agreed to reduce it further, but was unwilling to do so beyond a certain point. Our "fit" then began to widen a little. Dr. C had said that he had hoped that I would want to be his mentor. We knew that his theoretical bent, like mine, was toward contemporary ideas, so this was a good fit. Would I have been willing to reduce my fee further, he wondered, if he had chosen to apply to the contemporary institute? I felt Dr. C was, at least, testing whether I "needed" him to accommodate to this preference. I replied, "Possibly, but I'm not sure." I would have liked to be his mentor, but I was beginning to wonder whether too many specificities of mis-fit were emerging for this to happen.

Our analysis of these comprised a discovery in process of our needs and limitations in relation to each other. I was aware that the fee he stood by felt too low with respect to my own budget as well as to my sense of personal value. I also felt he needed me actually to be the kind of mother that he never had, the mother who would not only support his move to delineate from her, but also materially support him in that regard. And, unlike the mother, I should eschew the importance of money (to me, at least). I recognized that I was a little like his mother, though, insofar as I attached a certain importance to his willingness to monetarily value my "mentoring" a little higher by putting his money, as it were, where his declaration was.

With regret on both our parts, we could not find a "fit," and we parted, on amicable terms. It occurred to me later that part of his decision to find another training analyst may also have been due to his regarding my disinclination to lower my fees further as the "authority" of a mother to whom making money was central. I have since wondered, though, whether Dr. C may have experienced some therapeutic benefit from a "father" who could assert the value of what he had to offer.

The concepts of transference and countertransference do not quite do justice to the specificity of fits and misfits attending the process between

Dr. C and myself. Because Dr. C and I were able openly to talk about the specific complexities in our relationship (a capacity which, fortunately, was always one of our "fits"), we came to understand and appreciate each other's perspectives, the meaning to each other of our particular needs, positions taken, and limitations.

The crucial issues for this analysand were his experience of who his analyst *is*, in relation to him, and how this would affect who *he* needed to *become*. These issues emerged in the reciprocal specificity of our process. The patient's experience of the therapist as someone who was open to differing perspectives for understanding—including, of course, his own—was salutary, but it simultaneously left him without the sense of being connected to an idealizable authority. Perhaps, though, both of our capacities to respect differing perspectives came to transcend accommodative reactiveness, and he—and I—profited thereby from some optimally responsive time we spent together.

This case material also addresses the question about whether it is therapeutically optimal to the patient that the analyst "know" or "not know." Specificity theory illuminates how the experience of an analyst who is open to not knowing in one way may not be therapeutic for a particular analysand who does need him to be "knowing" in another way. Dr. C would appear to have needed me, in certain ways, to be both. He did not want someone who knew or could know what he wanted to pursue, rather, he wanted to choose pursuits in a world where something was known. There are levels of knowing. At the level of process, he needed me to "not know" with him, but at the level of response, he needed me to "know" which institute. Another way of putting this is that dynamism of discovery itself can, in a specific sense, be anathema or salutary to a particular patient. For this patient, it was anathema in one way, and in another was just what he needed.

Specificity theory also alters how we now apprehend a number of central concepts and principles in psychoanalysis, and has significant implications for how we utilize them in our work. In the next chapter, we focus on some of these, and illustrate them with more case material.

NOTES

1. We use the designations "psychoanalytic" and "psychodynamic" interchangeably.

2. "To fit life every time to a theory is in itself a mechanistic process . . . Theory as theory is all right. But the moment you apply it to *life*, especially to the subjective life, the theory becomes mechanistic, a substitute for life, a factor in the vicious unconscious" (D.H. Lawrence, 1936, in *Phoenix*, Vol. I, 1980, p. 378).

3. We also note that the concept, "transference," either in its classical definition as the bringing forward of childhood experience, or in its contemporary designation

as organizing activity, also does not do justice to the comparable determinants of who the *patient* is.

4. We are reminded, here, of the aphorism from 1 Corinthians 14:1–40, that "All our knowledge is partial . . . We know only in part and act constantly on the basis of incomplete information." According to the poet, Robert Frost, the ability to do so constitutes the definition of wisdom (referenced by Maurice Levine, in *Psychiatry and Ethics*, M. Levine, 1972, Publ. G. Braziller).

5. Attempts are being made to measure dark matter through its effect upon gravity.

6. See also Fiscalini (1994) who offers this as a new perspective for the Interpersonalist approach.

7. cf. Tronick's concept of "thickness," which we describe in chapter 8.

8. See also Ferenczi's analogous concept of elasticity within the psychoanalytic situation (Ferenczi, 1928).

9. For an interesting discussion on a related theme, see Lucyann Carlton's summary of the panel discussions of the 30th Annual International Conference on the Psychology of the Self: "Making Sense of Self and Systems in Psychoanalysis."

10. At that time, I was practicing in Toronto and was introducing self psychology to the psychoanalytic/psychotherapy community.

8

How Specificity Theory Alters Our View of Psychoanalytic Concepts and Principles and How This Affects Therapeutic Action

Specificity theory alters of our view of psychoanalytic concepts and principles, and how we use them. In some instances, specificity theory invites their re-conceptualization. To illustrate this, we will look at how *analyzability, transference, countertransference,* and *self-disclosure*[1] are transformed from the perspective of the specificity of process.

ANALYZABILITY

From the perspective of specificity theory, the question as to whether someone is "analyzable" changes radically. Indeed, it no longer remains a question at all. Rather than assessing the patient's capacity to utilize psychoanalytic treatment on the basis of traditionally stipulated criteria—such as psychological mindedness, substantial tolerance for frustration, capacity for free association as well as for good reality testing, which would exclude psychotic[2] or borderline conditions—the question becomes for analyst and analysand alike whether they can be together therapeutically. "Selection" for treatment is optimally mutual selection. Sperry (2007) reflects our view that "analyzability" is a systems issue, and agrees with Stolorow's (1988) assertion that "What must be assessed is the functioning of the entire Intersubjective system, the goodness of fit between what the patient most needs to have understood and what the analyst is capable of understanding" (p. 152). Sperry adds, "In determining analyzability, the question that needs to be asked is what does it take to make analysis viable for this particular analyst and patient at this time?"

We have, in fact, seen vivid illustrations of this challenge in the two cases described by Lucyann Carlton (in chapter 3, pp. 17–27). In the first one, Carlton, as analysand, struggled to circumvent her "unanalyzability" within an essentially classical analysis. In effect, when she did not respond to the embedded expectations within her analyst's interpretations, she was in danger, as it were, of becoming regarded as "unanalyzable." Carlton was unable to evoke the particular responsiveness she needed from her analyst as her analyst's theory precluded this. There was a specific mis-fit within the dyad that stymied the therapy, and the analyst employed what Eissler (1953) called a "parameter," the temporary departure from acceptable analytic practice—interpretive explication—in order to dislodge the patient's resistance or acting out, but which was abandoned as soon as the analyst could return to doing "proper" analysis. In the second situation, as analyst, working from the perspective of specificity theory, a different conceptualization of "analyzability," and different practice, emerged.

Specificity theory requires no recourse to the "parameter." Therapeutic possibility is neither generalizable according to traditional criteria for "analyzability," nor applicable on that basis with regard to assessment of the patient for treatment. The question is, rather, can that therapist and that patient work effectively together, and if not, why not? When "analyzability" with its assumption of analyst as authoritative expert is rejected, concerns of fit itself might become the focus of the analytic work, requiring exploration and possibly change by either analyst or analysand, or both.

One of the traditional adjuncts that used to be widely employed to enhance the assessment of patients for psychodynamic psychotherapy was to obtain projective tests such as the Rorschach and TAT on almost every patient. As I have become more aware of the power of the specificity of process as well as its unpredictable course with regard to the potential for therapeutic effect, I have no longer ordered these tests.

Here are two other illustrations of how specificity theory changes our view of "analyzability":

Illustration 1—Rick, Dr. D and Dr. Carlton

Dr. Carlton offers an example of a treatment where the shift from "analyzability" to "specificity of fit" was at the forefront in her supervision with Dr. D, who had recently started treatment of a young man with a history of acting out. When he felt that someone frustrated his goals, he would become aggressive and threatening, sometimes actually starting fights. And if he felt rejected by a woman, he would stalk her and seek secretly to frighten her in some way. However, with specificity theory as theoretical backdrop to the supervision, the work in the supervision did not focus upon whether Rick was analyzable, whether he had the ego strength to tolerate and benefit from an analysis. Rather, Dr. Carlton worked with Dr. D to assess, as best she could prospectively, whether her fit with Rick would allow for and support the therapeutic change that Rick sought. While this supervision was less focused on the specificity of the relationship between Dr. Carlton and Dr. D, as are the examples provided later in chapter 10, the specificity of the analytic relationship under analytic supervision was the focus. Dr. D sought supervision for a patient for whom the issue of their fit was of concern from the outset.

Initially, Dr. D entered supervision concerned about Rick's analyzability; the focus was on whether Rick had sufficient ego strength to tolerate an analysis. Dr. Carlton first listened to Dr. D's concerns. Rick was referred by his psychopharmacologist for five times a week analysis. He was a 32-year-old, single young man with a lifelong history of depression. He had recently been discharged from a hospitalization for a suicide attempt. He called it an "attempt," but this was so only because Rick did not die from the overdose of medication. He did not die, but not due to any failure of his. He had carefully and accurately discerned a type and an amount of medication that would be certainly lethal. He selected a time and place where any possibility of discovery was remote. He ingested the deadly potion. As Rick lapsed into unconsciousness, he had an unpredictable, idiosyncratic response to the medication that caused him to vomit most of it. However, for his part, he effected his suicide. Dr. D was very drawn to Rick. He presented as a very intelligent, charismatic young man, and was very motivated for treatment. He told his analyst at their first meeting, "My life is in ruins, but I have never been willing to admit it. I see, my suicide-survival has made me see, that I am the cause of my torment. I lost my white picket fence dream, but I did it. I have been in therapy for four years, once a week. I went every week. I never missed. I did my homework. But I did not ever really tell my therapist how I felt. I did not stop my self-destructive behaviors. I only got worse. I lost my friends, family, job, and the girl of my dreams. Now I know about Analysis. It is my only hope." He said all of this with the fervor of the converted. "I am going to tell you everything and I am changing the way that I have done things, now." At the same time, the analyst had been told by the referring psychiatrist that Rick had a significant history of stalking, and, indeed, even terrorizing past girlfriends, if he felt rejected or abandoned by a lover.

In their first session, Rick spoke of a dark, destructive despair that had enshrouded him most of his life. He felt ashamed and defective. He cycled from solitary desolation to expansive efficacy, from creative vision and charismatic leadership to destructive rages. He felt haunted by inchoate vengeful feelings and yearnings for intimacy as far back as he could remember. Dr. D was quite drawn to Rick's intensity of engagement, his apparent honesty in self-appraisal, and his capacity to reflect upon his internal states.

In the next several sessions, this patient spoke of his desire for a close, loving relationship with his mother, but that it had been hostile and combative since he was a little boy. At 13 years of age, his mother had arranged to have him kidnapped in the middle of the night to deliver him to a residential treatment center. He had been left in the residential treatment center until he graduated from high school. He had been closest with his father, who had committed suicide when Rick was only six years old. Rick believed that his mother's critical, cold demeanor had led to his father's drinking that had destroyed him.

During Dr. D's fourth session with Rick, the one that precipitated her decision to seek supervision, Rick spoke more of the rage that he suffered, and could not control, if he felt rejected by someone he desired. If someone disappointed him he felt intentionally humiliated or tormented. With this injury, he became so enraged that he became intent on revenge. He utilized his keen intellect to devise ways continuously to terrorize the other, without the risk of detection. He told of a young lady with whom he had arranged a date who had canceled at the last moment with some excuse that he did not believe to be true. With relish, he described to Dr. D his secret plot to ruin her in the eyes of her employer. He delighted in his ability to stalk another girl through repeated random threatening cell phone calls that could not be traced back to him. Though he had a restraining order issued against him, and he had served time in jail for these types of pursuits, he reported that these punishments only served to enhance his skill to evade detection. At the same time, as Rick spoke of these desires and behaviors, he did share them as problematic. He was tormented by his desire to torment. He reflected upon and shared his awareness that his feelings and his tactics were inappropriate. He told Dr. D, with conviction, that he was committed to never take these actions again. He had thrown away his cell phone and had not acted on these destructive desires. He was desperate to manage the intolerable feelings with which he suffered when he suppressed his need for revenge.

In the supervision with Dr. D, Dr. Carlton first focused on Dr. D's own feelings with Rick and her own history that might give some context to the unease that she felt with this patient. When Dr. D was an adolescent, her father had had a psychotic episode, believing that his daughter was poisoning him. As she sequestered herself in her bedroom to prepare for exams, her father would silently listen at the door for proof of her researching specific poisonous agents, lunging at her in rage if she unexpectedly tried to leave her room. Her developmentally expected individuation and separation during adolescence was interpreted by this psychotic father as personal abandonment, and, worse, desired annihilation of him by his daughter. For a period of time, Dr. D had been subjected to her father's stalking, paranoid fears, and unpredictable rages, to a degree that she could become anxious now, in her adult life, when she sensed someone was experiencing her as intending them harm.

Dr. D was drawn to work with Rick, particularly given Rick's own nascent awareness of the damage that his acting out created for him and his conviction to cease these behaviors. Rick seemed situated in his life where he might for the first time be able to obtain life-saving help through an analytic relationship. But in supervision, Dr. D became aware, as well, that as she listened to Rick's recounting of his stalking, she felt a familiar fear. As Rick described his surreptitious spying on one who had spurned him, memories of her father's stalking and paranoid rages began to feel more immediate.

The focus of the supervision was not whether Rick was analyzable, but whether she, Dr. D, had capacity to treat this young man. It was her vulnerability from her own history that was the center of supervision. The supervisory couple struggled with a dilemma. Dr. D desired to respond to this highly intelligent, motivated, and sensitive young man. At the same time, she feared her own fears would constrict her capacity to respond to him to a degree that the potential for a therapeutic relationship would be hindered from the outset. As Dr. Carlton and Dr. D explored Dr. D's feelings, Dr. D's fear that Rick might stalk her did not emerge as a significant worry for her. More significantly, she was concerned about the *unconscious* influence that her fear might exert on her capacity to be present to Rick in their ongoing daily interactions. Dr. Carlton and Dr. D both recognized that the unique confluence of Rick's history of stealth and stalking, with Dr. D's own history of a father who had stalked her created from the outset a relationship with significant potential restraint. She had spent years living with her father, being attuned unconsciously to her father's moods, altering her behavior to please him, and altering her behavior to avoid his irrational murderous rages. As an adolescent, her way of life, her way of being, was to monitor her father's possible interpretations of her movements, and alter them as she could, to avoid eliciting terrifying rages. There was for her a familiar, emotionally intense edginess in Rick that aroused this old, familiar vigilant state. In just the first several sessions, she sensed Rick's sensitivity to emotional injury and could feel her reflexive constriction in her responsiveness to him. At the same time, Rick had many qualities that would render analysis a most promising treatment for him. Rick's suicide attempt and subsequent treatment had developed a certain level of psychological awareness and motivation for treatment that was new for Rick. His rituals of retribution might not ever be evoked. With a different analyst, the fear of accusatory rage need not linger at the edge of the analysis, always constricting and constraining the two. Together, Dr. D and Dr. Carlton understood that Rick was now possessed of a new resolve to alter his behavior and appreciated the emergent strength of his ability to reflect on his feelings. Nevertheless, Dr. D concluded for herself that the felt intensity of his emotional sensitivity to rejection and his immediate, reflexive need to injure the one who had wounded him, despite his commitment to not act upon this need, was so intense at this time that she was too anxious to be an effective analyst for him.

With her conclusion that she was not the best analyst for Rick, she shared with him, "I do not feel that I am strong enough to be a good analyst for you. I suspect that as we work together, over time, I would become very aware of the ways that you might experience me as intentionally tormenting or rejecting. I am concerned that I might, because of my own personal history, unconsciously alter my behavior to avoid evoking these feelings in you. My attempts to avoid your anger and feelings of rejection and abandonment might not allow you to have experiences that you need in your therapeutic work."

Let's take a closer look at this assessment of "analyzability" through the lens of the specificity of dyadic process. Although this analyst felt drawn to Rick—he was intelligent, professionally successful, motivated for analysis, psychologically minded and ready to share his inner world—Dr. D found herself responding to Rick's intensity and vulnerability to rejection and abandonment with cautious restraint.

In this analyst's appraisal of whether to undertake an analysis with Rick, she struggled with whether she could treat him. However, she neither regarded him as "unanalyzable" on the basis of traditional criteria, nor on the basis of the traditional consideration of this situation in terms of transference-countertransference interaction. Rather, with specificity theory as the perspective in the supervision, it was incumbent upon the analyst rigorously to question her capacity to treat this young man. This theory placed *the analyst, and her abilities as an analyst for Rick,* at the center of her consideration of therapeutic possibility.

The supervisorial focus and the analyst's decision were based on a consideration of therapeutic possibility in a fundamentally different way from one based upon traditional psychoanalytic theory. It required *this analyst* bringing to the fore an examination of the particular way that *she* might or might not be able to work optimally with *this particular patient.* That is, working with specificity theory required the analyst to assume the uncomfortable obligation to examine possible limitations on her capacity to respond therapeutically to him, in the specificity of their process. Her own limitations and capabilities vis-à-vis this patient were thus at the center of her examination rather than defined criteria, based upon structurally defined theory, against which to assess the patient's treatability.

Illustration 2—Dina, the Demons, and Dr. B

In apparent contrast to the above case, my acceptance of Dina for psychoanalytic treatment also demonstrates how the concept of "analyzability" looks so very different from the perspective of specificity theory. Dina was referred to me at age 45 by Dr. A, a self psychologically oriented psychiatrist who had treated her several years ago when Dina was living in Albany. Dr. A told me that Dina had had several hospitalizations for what was likely a bipolar disorder. My impression, though, after seeing Dina for a few weeks, was that a paranoid schizophrenic process had somehow gone unrecognized. Dr. A conveyed that Dina would be helped if I just listened to her quietly for daily sessions, as he had done over a period of some two years. While I was aware, as a psychiatrist, that there were prescribed treatments for both disorders, as an analyst whose work was being increasingly influenced by specificity theory, I was prepared to find out how I might be of help, at this time, in ways that might or might not include treatments that are traditionally prescribed for her illness, or how Dr. A had worked with her.

In our initial telephone conversation, Dina told me that she had recently been having some difficulty with her current therapist, Dr. K. She had no confidence in either him or in her psychopharmacologist. She felt that they were being negatively influenced by some outsiders to turn against her. She also conveyed her worry that I might be frightened by this. I conveyed to Dina that I was not feeling frightened, but that it sounded to me that she felt scared. She agreed; and I later learned from Dr. A that Dina had welcomed this response. In reflecting on what had significantly transpired between us in this interchange, I realized I had been able to respond to Dina's need for a relationship in which I would not be put off by her experience of a frightening, threatening world.

We arranged an appointment. With regard to Dina's personal history, I will just mention, for the purposes of my illustration, that her mother was for many years depressed and self-preoccupied from the time Dina was two, and that in later years her mother became very controlling and intrusive. Her father tended to be inappropriately intimate with her as a child, though apparently not overtly sexual. As a teenager, he would mock her adolescent idiom, and in her young adulthood, would put a damper on any interest she might show in a man. Yet, Dina also felt him to be her protector, and caregiver, which I suspected constituted more of a creative fantasy than a lived experience. Her mother was still alive; her father had died several years ago.

When I met Dina for our first session, I felt an immediate liking for her. I was drawn to her direct, friendly way of relating to me, although her demeanor had an oddly wooden quality to it.

Dina described her disillusionment with previous therapists and others in her life whom she had trusted, who "turned" on her—people who were revealed to be in one way or another bad or threatening. She seemed quite anxious that I believe everything she was saying. She had become terribly upset when former therapists to whom she spoke of these dangers told her that she was paranoid and must be on medication. She had acceded to taking a small dose of zyprexa, though, which did relieve her anxiety somewhat at times. Initially, Dina appeared satisfied that I just listened respectfully to her, and was relieved that I did not feel the need to have her medication reassessed at this time.

In this first consultation, Dina told me about several ways in which I also fell short. She was expecting someone younger, and who dressed more conservatively, in a shirt with a tie, and she was not especially happy that I charged a fee, and that I really *was* older than she preferred. She also told me, a bit later on, that I was not sweet like her first psychiatrist, Dr. A, that she needed sweets when she left our sessions. She also thought I was gay. Why? Well, that was unclear. Having a dog in the room was some evidence for that. Despite my several flaws, Dina wanted to work with me and, at her request, we began to meet for five sessions a week, face-to-face.

Let us consider how specificity theory, whose central perspective entails a shift from structure to the specificity of process, affected my view that Dina would be "treatable."

Despite the unquestionable fact that Dina had a major psychiatric disorder that psychoanalysts tend to regard as not treatable by that method, and that those who do offer certain prescriptive protocols,[3] I was not thinking primarily in these ways. I was, rather, finding myself experiencing Dina as a person who was looking, quite anxiously, for a trustable, close therapeutic relationship. I felt moved to respond to Dina with regard to what she seemed to be looking for from me, yet in working from the perspective of specificity theory, I could not know whether I could help her, or in what ways, or what we might accomplish together. I only knew that I was not going to assume that what I might optimally offer Dina was to just listen, ensure she take the right drugs, or interpret primitive psychotic defenses in the context of her paranoid-schizoid organization. Yet I was prepared to respond in any of those ways, if it became apparent as our process emerged that these, or indeed other responses whose possible utility I could not anticipate—and that I could offer—might optimally promote therapeutic experience for her. I found myself moving toward this troubled, frightened, and somewhat strange lady who believed I could help her.

Dina and I got on well together; in particular, the atmosphere of the treatment was initially one of warm trust, wherein Dina frequently conveyed her gratitude for what she experienced as my care and helpfulness. Within a few months, Dina began to take steps in her life that she never imagined she could. Foremost amongst them were practical plans, after many years, to rejoin her golf club, which would entail a struggle to make friends with some very difficult ladies—all of which she actually did. She also began to resume her interest in clothes, shopping, and in art, and she discussed with me at length what she was doing in these areas.

What was emerging between us, despite my shortcomings and her formal diagnosis, was a sense of a specificity of fittedness, in interesting ways. I have come to learn that my empathic antennae are particularly attuned to the specificity of needed responsiveness with regard to relational intimacy—one might say, I have a sort of valence for this, which ranges from recognition of a patient's need for utter privacy to embracing depths of need for personal mutuality. As far as I know, this does not reflect any formalized structure theory; but it does, of course, have a good deal to do with issues of trust. I sensed that Dina moved widely as well as shakily on this spectrum, and her apparent trust in me drew me to her. I moved to Dina's somewhat naïve quality of openness and hopefulness about what we could do together, and with her belief that, despite my evident failings, I might be able to help her, perhaps even a bit better than some of the other therapists she had encountered out there. That was also, of course, appealing. Apart from the fact that I tend to "believe," as well as to believe in, my patients fully (which makes me a terrible therapist for psychopaths and pathological liars) I, like Dina, also like to believe I can trust someone who might not be entirely trustworthy but to whom I would be special and who would not let me down. While I am not so naïve that I believe this can always happen, I am, also like Dina, inclined to be hopeful, even when there may be some significant evidence that weighs to the contrary. I felt we made a warm connection in which we both felt we could work well together. I felt admiration for Dina for her pursuit of an elusive sense of stability, safety, and concern in a dangerous world in relation to which she appeared to me to be exquisitely vulnerable.

Sessions with Dina began to reveal her desperate wish to trust someone out there in a world that was inhabited by all forms of destructively invasive demonic-like entities that were assaulting her in viciously physical, excruciatingly painful, ways. In psychiatric terms, Dina was suffering intensely from persecutory delusions and hallucinations in virtually every sensory modality. Dina seemed to recognize that her perceptions and experiences were unusual, yet she experienced them as entirely real; and she conveyed to me that it was crucial to her that I believed they were factually true.[4] Not that I simply believe that she was *experiencing* all this as real—which I could and did—but that I, too, recognize, as she did, that everything she was describing was actually happening. Our discovery that I was having difficulty with that kind of validation constituted a limitation in relation to Dina's need which I could not have anticipated and that turned out to be pivotal for the continuation of the treatment beyond a certain point.

Early on, Dina revealed to me that she had a "friend"—"the friend," as she called him—whom she initially trusted implicitly (but who mysteriously later betrayed her) who was trying to protect her from these demons. I found both self psychological and Kleinian concepts to be variously useful in our process. I attempted to validate Dina's experience of the demons, and interpreted her use of unconscious splitting in the transference with regard to both them and "the friend." The latter sort of interpretation evoked confirmatory associations. The former—my attempts at validation—seemed to be more usable by Dina, even as I struggled to provide the particular kind of validation of them that Dina desperately pleaded for. What especially helped at one juncture, when Dina was beginning to miss some sessions, was my interpreting to her that I felt her difficulty in coming to see me and her belief in what her friend could do for her were related. That is, because she had been let down so much in her life, and was now experiencing me as someone who understood her, she was terribly frightened of taking a chance to throw her lot in with me, and that that is where her friend came in. Somewhat to my surprise, Dina not only quite agreed with this, she shared more of her feelings. She said she has been so disappointed by everyone; she has been so lonely. And that her fear had a lot to do with becoming involved with me. I acknowledged that insofar as she was beginning to feel that she was wanting this sort of thing with me, she was fearful that she was facing inevitable disappointment. She told me that it was hard for her that the therapy comprised only 45 minutes and that when she goes, she doesn't have me, that is, that therapy will not bring her what she longs for. She has really wanted to stay with me, even felt she wanted to move in with me.

Dina continued to convey how grateful she was for our work, that I had helped her to feel differently about herself and that it was a tragedy that she had not met me earlier in her life when she might have been able to benefit from the work we were doing, in particular, to find a man and have a normal life. And now, for the first time, she angrily linked the experiences of her demonic invaders with her experience of her mother, who doesn't listen to her, but rather impinges herself on Dina without any regard for what she wants and doesn't want, all of which Dina conveyed she had been struggling with, within herself, in relation to her mother all her life. But now, her body was so destroyed by these demons, that nothing could be done.

Dina's anxiety and pain—both psychic and somatic—became relentless and unbearable—and she began more and more often to speak of suicide as a way of ending them. At the same time, though, she reiterated the "reality" of her friend, and that of the dangers out there—dangers the nature of which no one, including me, would believe. However much I tried to "validate" (and I framed this in every way I could think of), I could not find a way to convey to Dina what she required—that I truly believed the actuality of her persecutory experiences (which I didn't).[5] It was not sufficient that I appreciated how much she needed this kind of validation—which, from the perspective of self psychology theory, might be regarded as a deep going need for alterego or twinship connection—nor was I able to "provide" it. I also did not feel I could enter her world as "play," as I have done, usefully, with other patients, in grim situations. "Playing" with this did not feel at all possible, for Dina, nor for me. Dina was deadly serious about her persecutory pain, and she continued to suffer terribly. Dina began to feel hopeless, but refused to take medication. She pleaded with me to help her end the unbearable pain the demons were causing her by helping her to end her life. This I could not do either, and Dina made a suicide attempt which necessitated her being admitted to hospital. Although she was not at all happy that I put her in there[6] and felt that I had betrayed her in doing so, when she came out of hospital, she expressed her wish to resume sessions with me. However, she was still suicidal, was refusing to take medication, and was determined to live with her controlling yet evidently quite dangerously unreliable mother. And I then discovered more of my limitations in context. I had to convey to Dina that I felt too anxious about her safety to resume seeing her under these conditions.

I have presented this vignette in some detail in order to illustrate how holding a theory of therapeutic specificity affects possibilities for treatment. Rather than assessing the patient's "analyzability" on the basis of criteria referable to the patient or to her diagnosis, both participants continue to engage a process of trying to find out whether they can—and, if so, how they can—be together therapeutically.

I have had various reactions to the dénouement of this case. Some of the most interesting responses have come from participants (senior analytic candidates and colleagues) participating in a case seminar I led at the Institute of Contemporary Psychoanalysis in Los Angeles. One member of the seminar reported how a colleague of his dealt with a "very difficult to believe" situation by saying something to the patient like, "I don't quite *get* what you're telling me, but I want to; let's go on, and maybe I will." I said that this sounded to me like a potentially very good response, yet it still would have felt to me like I was being disingenuous. I knew I could not actually come around to "getting" it. Dina needed to know that I knew her perceptions and her experiences were real. Her need was quite specific, and my ability to respond was specifically insufficient. One of the senior candidates in the seminar appeared to apprehend the nature of my struggle, and described a case of her own where her patient's experience was "close to unbelievable," "yet perhaps plausible" which, she thought, might have been what enabled her to offer her patient the responsiveness she seemed to feel was adequate. We agreed that the difference in the degree of our perception of plausibility could make a difference for us.

Another participant in the seminar described how a "companion of Faulkner's," in order to preserver Faulkner's goodwill and mood of expansiveness, had to acknowledge the existence of the home of Clem Snopes (an imaginary character who figures in one of Faulkner's novels), in a barren meadow that Faulkner was pointing out to him. She conveyed that, for Faulkner, this willingness of his companion to succumb to the reality he had created in fiction would seem to have been the acid test for a "new relationship." She added that she did not know whether she could do this sort of thing; but she believed that a person with delusions of persecution, plagued by devils, demands that we accept this version of reality and that, given what we know of toxic parents, this "metaphor" is indeed the reality some people must endure. My response was that I appreciated that she could not know whether she could do this, but there was an aspect of Dina's subjectivity with which she was truly at variance; and that it was somewhat like mine. For us it could be a metaphor, but for Dina it was not. It was truth, whose validation as such was essential for her. She could not, as it were, endure her experience, and I could not accept it as truth in the way she required, which might have helped.

Then, another member of the seminar offered her sense of something about me that may have stood in the way of my finding a way to do something more—that I appeared to place a high value on "integrity." It occurred to me later that this might be a euphemistic way of observing that I may have been unconsciously shackled by this value, in effect, by who I am in this regard. Is it possible that such a value was somehow evoked in that context, and that if it were not, I might have found some way to "be with" Dina in her "truth"? I was, at some level, gripped by the importance of "truth," as I saw it, just as Dina was, as she saw it. My afterthought was: Would it have been useful to put this possibility on the table, if I'd seen it then? Dina and I did what *we* could together (one might perhaps "validly" add, with her mother there, with whom neither of us could do anything, which may be another important part of our story, as yet untold).

Another student wrote to me after the seminar that what I described summed up for him the power and limits with regard to the specificity of analyst and patient. His only concern was that critics of the Theory would draw attention to its implying the removal of hope. "What if the bonding between patient and analyst never works, and the patient goes through an unending series of endings with dozens of analysts?" He thought that the patient might find the right analyst, but he wondered whether, when offering this vignette, I might undercut the potential criticism with some statement of hope for the patient, now. I thanked my colleague for this, and replied that I, too, leaned toward hope; yet, I added, I was recently thinking of adding as subtitle for the book the phrase "How Therapy Happens—*Or Does Not*" (a version of which I actually came to use). I told him I thought this reflected a more complete reality of psychoanalytic practice, which specificity theory describes.

The central, relevant question is not one of "analyzability," or "treatability," but rather of what constitutes the capacity of that particular dyad, in process, of being together therapeutically. I told him about my recent experience interviewing Ms. D., a woman who was contemplating a third analysis. She felt that her first two analyses were a failure, as she felt she had to terminate them when she experienced the inexplicable, but complete, loss of feeling for the analyst. She told me that if this one (the third one, now, which she was considering undertaking with me) failed, she would regard herself as unanalyzable. I responded by saying to her that I did not agree with the assumption that if analysis with the next person did not work, it was because of some flaw within herself. I added that I hoped that, if we agreed to work together, we would discover a way to do better, or if not, find out why we couldn't. In my discussion with the student, I learned that his view of the basis for a successful treatment was the establishment of a "bond," which entailed an assumption of the universal relevance of a particular structure theory. In a further interview with the prospective analysand, I learned that she did not have difficulty establishing a strong bond with her analysts. We discovered, rather, that she appeared to have a problem maintaining the intensity of her positive feelings, because of her sense of the analyst's inability to adequately match them, and that the resulting loss of feeling was intolerable to her.

I recalled, then, that when I'd presented my work with Dina at a major psychoanalytic conference, an experienced and respected colleague kept pressing me, "Couldn't you have done *something*?!"—that is, to preclude this outcome. I sensed that her question came from a place of hope, but also from a Weltanshauung of what "one" could do. It took some discussion before I was able to get across the idea that it was indeed a question of whether *I* could have done something else. Perhaps process with her, or with some other therapist, conceivably might have led to a different outcome, but this is what was possible for Dina and me, within the specificity of our dyad and in relation to its complex adjacent systems. After the presentation was over, as my colleague and I left the room, still talking, she reluctantly conceded, "You have made your point."

Sometimes, a degree of "thin slicing" (see chapter 7) can alert us in advance to stresses that we anticipate will exceed our capacity to manage therapy with a particular patient—as in Dr. Carlton's situation with Rick; but if this specificity is not evident, are we justified in generalizing that any particular illness, even such as the one from which Dina suffered, should determine a priori whether and if so, how, treatment should proceed? Dr. B and Dina could not know how their process would unfold. A specificity theory sensibility offers expanded opportunity for therapeutic experience, as Dr. Carlton's process with Beth vividly shows. Yet, we must also face a difficult "truth"—that regardless of how well a therapist has been analyzed, supervised, or continues to engage in ongoing consultation, she and her patient may encounter places that they are unable to move through safely or effectively as they explore the potentially therapeutic possibilities of their process. Dina and I actually worked remarkably well together for some time, until we bumped into specific limitations that reflected who we were with each other in our process—which, sadly, prevented us from traveling further than we did.

TRANSFERENCE AND COUNTERTRANSFERENCE

An analysis of a problematic therapeutic situation considering the specificity of the dyad not only goes well beyond conceptualization of the difficulty as "transference—countertransference"; it also illustrate how specificity theory alters our understanding of these terms themselves and their utility for clinical practice.

The concepts, transference and countertransference, have been central to psychoanalysis from its earliest days (Freud, 1912a) yet the delineation of what they represent has changed in a number of ways over time. Specificity theory adds a new perspective to how we consider them and how we use them.

The terms, transference and countertransference, are variously used to designate: (a) attitudes and feelings that patient and therapist have, respectively, toward each other that they bring forward from earlier life; and (b) all the feelings and attitudes experienced by each toward each other. The experiences that the terms denote are also understood as being variously evoked by the other.[7]

Freud at first regarded transference, which he used exclusively in the first way, as an almost insurmountable obstacle to effective treatment, but he soon came to apprehend it as an immensely important aspect of therapeutic work (see Bird, 1972). Racker (1968), like Heimann (1950) and Fosshage (1995), defines countertransference "as the totality of the analyst's psychological response to the patient" (p. 136), but distinguishes between "concordant" and "complementary" countertransference, the former being "the approximate union or identity between the various parts . . . of the subject and the object," the latter referring to "an object relationship . . . a 'real' transference in which the analyst 'repeats' previous experiences, the patient representing internal objects of the analyst" (p. 136). Natterson (1991) regards the concept, countertransference, as "too limited for a full understanding of a therapist's idiosyncratic contributions" (p. 42).[8] In practice, psychoanalysts tend to regard transference and countertransference as mainly associated with phenomena that may impede the flow of the treatment, and whose understanding may promote it (see Blum, 1986).

Self psychology theory introduced different ways of apprehending the meaning of these concepts and how they may be implicated in the treatment process. Kohut (1971) formulated the idea of selfobject transferences (though he perhaps more accurately recognized them as "transferencelike," p. 25) which the patient mobilizes in an attempt to restitute developmental disruption or arrest. The selfobject transferences denote experiences of mirroring, idealizing, and twinship on the part of the analysand in relation to the analyst. Kohut (1971); Kohut and Wolf (1978) also described selfobject countertransferences as the analyst's reactions to selfobject transferences. Stolorow & Atwood (1992) have distinguished between the selfobject, or developmental, dimension of transference and its repetitive dimension; and Marian Tolpin (2002) analogously developed Kohut's notion of the "leading edge" (ibid., p. 167), which alludes to selfobject experience, into "forward edge transferences" (ibid.), elaborating Kohut's emphasis on the salutary function of such experience for the development of the self. Tolpin distinguished these from "trailing edge pathology" (ibid., p. 169), which alludes to the repetitive dimension of transference.

STRUCTURE THEORY AND PROCESS THEORY

As Carlton has described (see chapter 2), all theories of therapy are premised upon a theory of mind, and that a fundamental distinction among theories can be drawn from their definitional essence of the nature of the mind either as *structure* or as *process*. All the characterizations of "transference" and "countertransference" that we have just outlined comprise concepts of formal theory that is primarily "structured." Such theory can be contrasted with theory conceived at the level of "process."

A structure theory assumes that the analyst can learn *about* the mind of another through cause-and-effect, linear reasoning. *Structure* theories comprise those familiar to us as classical psychoanalysis, ego-psychology, object relations theory, Kleinian, or self psychology theory, etc. In contrast, a theory of therapy that privileges *process* defines the mind as process that is always in process. Examples of such theories are intersubjective systems theory, complexity theory, and specificity theory.

Theories in which structured concepts are central offer definitive and universally applicable ways of understanding the patient, from which arise prescriptive and proscriptive guidelines for responding therapeutically. That is, defining the nature of the mind as *structure* or *process* has important implications for how our theories affect our practice.

Natterson (1991) has drawn attention to Ferenczi's implicit recognition, in his diary (Ferenczi, 1928), of the "continuous and crucial intersubjective process in every psychoanalytic therapy" (Natterson, p. 24). In 1939, Michael Balint and Alice Balint took what was at that time a radical step toward a process, or systems, approach to psychoanalytic theory and practice when they explicitly made the assertion that "the analytical situation is the result of an interplay between the patient's transference and the analyst's counter-transference, complicated by the reactions released in each by the other's transference onto him" (p. 226). They suggested, in effect, that transference and countertransference should be mutually addressed in process. Stolorow and his colleagues (1987) have recast the meaning of transference and countertransference in ways that offer a particular kind of bi-directional conceptualization. Intersubjective systems theory comprehends transference and countertransference as manifestations of the "organizing activity" of analysand and analyst, respectively—the ways in which the experience by each of the analytic relationship is shaped by his or her "archaically determined configurations of self and object . . ." (Stolorow,

Atwood, & Brandchaft, 1987, p. 36). "Transference and countertransference together form an intersubjective system of reciprocal mutual influence" (p. 42).

Specificity theory, too, offers a process, or systems, conceptualization of transference and countertransference. Specificity theory, however, draws attention to the uniqueness of each analytic dyad and the specificity of the process of its particular participants. Specificity theory holds that psychoanalytic treatment reflects the operation of a quintessentially unique reciprocal process for each analyst-patient couple, in effect, a system which may be complexly affected by other systems, both adjacent and distant. This is a different way of talking about what most analysts still apprehend as transference and countertransference, terms we regard as mechanistic metaphors, which have become too narrow, circumscribed and linear in their approach. We would, rather, regard who each of the particular participants is, and becomes, in the specificity of their interaction.

In 1996, Peter Thomson and I (Bacal & Thomson, 1996) drew attention to a new view of transference and countertransference from the perspective of self psychology in the context of disruption. We suggested replacing the concept, "countertransference," with that of the analyst's experience of frustration of *particular* selfobject needs of his own that emerged in relation to the patient. In other words, we offered a different way of apprehending the analyst's experience of reactive selfobject disruption in relation to the analysand. This, in effect, entailed replacing the term, "countertransference," with a mixed-model concept that comprised a structured concept within self psychology: the analyst's reaction to the frustration of his selfobject needs, along with the specificity of the analyst's experience as it emerged in process. Moving more toward a process perspective, we then (Bacal & Thomson, 1998) offered the term, "*relatedness reaction*" (p. 254), as a more accurate way of representing problematic *interaction*.

Quite apart from constituting essentially single-body terms connoting the operation of one party's attitudes and feelings being directed at the other, *transference* and *countertransference* do not adequately represent the variable specificity of the disruptions that they signify. That is, while these terms may emerge in process with understandable, and apparently useful, relational relevance, they delimit to defined experience the understanding of phenomena to which they refer within the uniqueness of that particular dyad. From the perspective of specificity theory, therefore, I would now change the term, *relatedness reaction* to *the specificity of relational disruption.*

That is, specificity theory draws attention to the *particularity* of process in understanding disruptive experience within the dyad. It emphasizes the importance of the fluid, reciprocal influence within the particular dyadic system (and influences on it from without). It especially draws attention to the unique specificities that emerge within the patient-therapist dyadic process that may be disturbing the treatment, and whose recognition may have important therapeutic potential. Unlike the designations, transference and countertransference, though, the perspectives of specificity theory do not presume what particular processes may be determining the disruption.

The two clinical examples we offered earlier (of Rick, Dr. D and Dr. Carlton, and of Dina, Dr. B and the Demons) to illustrate how analyzability looks so very different from the perspective of specificity theory, also extensively depict how our understanding of "transference" and "countertransference" changes thereby.

Here are two further examples:

Patricia and Dr B

Patricia and I were aware of her vulnerability to separation, yet we did not anticipate the severity of the disruption consequent upon the difficulty in maintaining reliable contact when I was on vacation in a faraway land for several weeks. Both analyst and analysand recognized the intense and very early nature of her attachment, which had developed in their seven times a week analysis. The analyst had hoped that the arrangement he had set up for them to be in regular contact by e-mail and cell phone would suffice, but neither e-mail nor cell-phone service provided adequate or reliable contact. The sustained absence of the analyst in the context of an analysis that had offered frequent, reliable presence of the analyst, triggered a traumatic state for Patricia. She was dropped into a terrible abyss where she experienced an almost continuous and virtually unbearable agony of traumatic abandonment. I understood the plight of my patient, as well as her pain, and tried everything I could to maintain contact with her through the frustratingly flawed communications systems available at the time between southeast Asia and the western United States. I also found myself facing understandable distress and anger on the part of my wife at having her vacation experience repeatedly interfered with by my frequent attempts to be in touch with my patient.

Within the system constituted by analyst and analysand, the disruption, from the patient's side, derived from the reactivation of unmanageable early experiences of utter desertion. While the analyst continued to feel committed to respond to his patient's frantic need to be connected, he also experienced continual strain as he could do little to relieve either his patient's desperation or his wife's disturbance. The adjacent systems that impacted their attempts to connect—the abysmal communications system and the anger and disappointment on the part of the analyst's wife—intensified the already tense *relationally specific disruptions* within their process. These disruptions emerged as specific not only to each individual within their dyadic process but also in respect of how each dyad reciprocally impacted the other.

To account for the analysand's or the analyst's experience, either in the primary situation or/and occasioned by the impact on them by outside circumstances, solely by reference to the traditionally configured concepts of transference and countertransference, is to delimit our understanding of the specific and complex determinants of what was transpiring. A traditional formulation would have us attend solely to the patient's experience in terms of transference onto the analyst of the patient's recurrent experiences of abandonment and severe letdown by both parents in very early childhood; and that she was terrified and enraged consequent upon her re-experiencing these in relation to her analyst when he violated her expectations (see Lachmann, 2008) when he was, not infrequently, "not there" when the e-mail or phone connection was significantly faulty, especially when the phone connection would abruptly disappear. According to the classical formulation, he was having a "countertransference reaction" of guilt-laden anxiety to the patient's transference—as well as to his wife's disapproval, which in part derived from his constant failure to behave in the "right" way toward his patient as the mother of his childhood when her upset could not be ameliorated by his inadequate accommodation to her emotional requirements.

While all of this may be valid, to apprehend what was transpiring through the conceptual lens of transference and countertransference, even if we regard them as the clash of differently organized subjectivities, does not do justice to their specificity. In this terribly difficult situation, *they did whatever they could to make it work. Both analyst and analysand faced a complexity of determinants specific to who they were in relation to each other in their process, which was reciprocally affected and intensified by the impact of outside systems in ways and to extents that exceeded their capacity to remedy them adequately.*

Dr. Sandler and the Schoolteacher

In his remarkable 1976 article, "Countertransference and Role-Responsiveness," Joseph Sandler[9] apprehends transference and countertransference in a way that approaches the perspective of the specificity of process. Sandler suggests that in certain instances, there is a more accurate way of apprehending the analyst's behavior toward the patient than how it is traditionally understood, that is, as the analyst's countertransference reaction to the patient's transference, entirely derived from within himself. Sandler considers that it could more usefully be seen as "a *compromise* between the analyst's own tendencies or propensities and the role-relationship which the patient is unconsciously seeking to establish" (p. 47).

Sandler describes a patient, a schoolteacher in her late 20s, who regularly cried during her analytic sessions, in response to which he would always offer her a Kleenex. One day he found himself not offering his patient a Kleenex when she began to cry, and she reacted with anger and panic. "What emerged then was material which lent a great deal of *specificity* to something which we had not been able to crystallize previously" (our emphasis). The patient's further associations revealed that "her great need for control and for structures in her life was based on a fear that she should would soil or wet herself *and that there would not be an adult around to clean her up.*" This turned out to be a fear constituting "a specific fantasy . . . which dominated her life from early childhood under the impact of the mother's withdrawal from her because of the birth of a second child." "I think," Sandler writes, "that I must have picked up unconscious cues from the patient which prompted me to behave in a certain way in her analysis, both to keep passing her the tissues and then to omit doing so." Sandler reflects that, in the session, he was not around to ensure she was clean, just as she experienced her mother not being there for her after the birth of her brother, to clean her, as she was too busy attending to the new baby. Sandler suggests that, in this analytic process, "a complicated *system* of unconscious cues, both given and received, [was] involved" (italics added). The discovery, in this way, of this fantasy and its working through "marked a crucial point in [this patient's] analysis." Although Sandler does not tell us what was evoked within himself in the interaction with his patient, his reference to "the analyst's own tendencies and propensities" suggests that he was aware that a shared specificity between analyst and analysand significantly contributed to what was happening within their process.

SELF-DISCLOSURE

Many practitioners now recognize that the response of sharing their subjectivity with patients can be useful. They regard this, however, as a special kind of therapeutic action, called "self-disclosure," which is either prescribed or proscribed according to one structure theory or another. In this section, we examine some universally formulated declarations about whether it is therapeutically optimal for the analyst to share his subjectivity with the patient; for example, does this impede or facilitate the emergence of transference (the underlying assumption being that the latter is always therapeutic)? Are there workable guidelines for "self-disclosure," as Maroda (2010) asserts? From the perspective of specificity theory, our view of "self-disclosure" changes: the sharing of the analyst's subjectivity with the patient is not regarded a "special" response on the part of the analyst, which the term, self-disclosure, connotes.

The traditional psychoanalytic position is that the analyst should never "self-disclose," as this is thought to interfere with the elaboration of fantasy, both conscious and unconscious, and to impede the unfolding of transference. The perspective of classical psychoanalysis on the analyst's' sharing his subjectivity with the patient constitutes a good example of proscriptive responsiveness, based upon a (very well known) structure theory.

Freud, (1912b) regarded the avoidance of self-disclosure to be necessary for the development and resolution of a transference neurosis. "The resolution of transference . . . is made more difficult by an intimate attitude on the doctor's part" (p. 118). Freud provides clear guidelines. "The doctor should be opaque to the patient and . . . show them nothing but what is shown to him" (p. 118). Freud (1915) concludes, "the treatment must be carried out in abstinence" (p. 165). Freud (1912b) explicitly warns against self-disclosure. "Young and eager psychoanalysts will no doubt be tempted to bring their own individual feeling into the discussion in order to carry the patient along with them and lift him over the barrier of his own narrow personality" (p. 117). "[T]his technique," he continues, "achieves nothing towards the uncovering of what is unconscious to the patient . . . in severer cases it invariably fails by encouraging the patient to be insatiable" (p. 118). As Rosenblum (1998, p. 538) puts it, "Freud (1919) believed that need and longing for gratification from the analyst are what impel the analysand to do the analytic work. Gratification had to be withheld. Because he thought that self-disclosure by the analyst was a form of gratification,[10] it was to be avoided."

In his prologue to the issue of *Psychoanalytic Inquiry* devoted to contemporary perspectives on this theme, Michael Miletic (1998) presents Rosenblum's perspective on self-disclosure—the analyst speaking about himself/herself in a more natural way, including the sharing of his own thoughts and feelings in an active attempt to engage the patient emotionally in an analytic stalemate. This, in effect, is a guideline based in effect upon a particular structure theory, in this case, that sharing one's subjectivity is a good thing to do in an impasse. We are reminded here of Eissler's notion of the parameter (1953)—a definitive technical guideline based upon classical theory—that any apparently necessary departure from standard (in this case, classical) technique be abandoned as soon as possible, so that the analyst may resume proper analytic work as soon as possible.

Miletic (1998) endorses Owen Renik's recommendation that the analyst share his subjectivity with the patient. According to Renik, "the principle of analytic anonymity encourages idealization of the analyst as an authoritative observer of reality within the treatment situation" (Renik, 1995, p. 477). Renik suggests that we not only discard it but also contradict it (p. 481). Renik's assertions appear to be based on the theory that the analyst's assuming a position of authority is ubiquitously anti-therapeutic. Renik advocates both dispossessing the patient of the expectation that the analyst will not self-disclose, and of always telling the patient why he is doing so.[11]

There is something to be said for questioning the authoritativeness of any principle if practice renders it doubtful, but it is also useful to be wary of universalizing what is optimally therapeutic for the patient. As the examples of Dr. C and Dr. B, in chapter 7, illustrate, the specific complexities of an analysand's need to idealize the analyst as an authority, along with the capacity and limits of the particular analyst to respond optimally to these needs, challenge the usefulness of prescribing or proscribing based upon any structure theory. Our patients experience a wide variety of modes and kinds of responsiveness as optimally therapeutic (Bacal, 1985, 1998).[12] This also applies to the question of whether the analyst should share his subjectivity with the patient—so-called self-disclosure. From the perspective of specificity theory, the analyst's sharing his subjective experience with the patient is just one response among many that, in any particular instance, may or may not be therapeutic for that patient, and possible for that analyst.

Therapists who identify themselves with the American Relational School have been especially interested in exploring the usefulness of self-disclosure, partly because they place a high therapeutic value upon mutuality and reciprocity (Aron, 1996), as well as upon the importance of responding with regard to the discreteness of the two participants in the treatment situation, in contrast to self psychologists who have been inclined to privilege responses that focus on the patient's subjectivity that may blur the psychological distinction between self and other.[13] Fosshage, a self psychologist, has, in effect, described interactions with a particular patient that reveal the unpredictability of the therapeutic usefulness of self-disclosure when considered a priori from the perspective of any particular structured theory (Fosshage, 1998), in this case, self psychology or relational theory. Fosshage has described interactions with a particular patient that reveal the unpredictability of the therapeutic usefulness of self-disclosure when considered from the perspective of a particular structured theory (Fosshage, 1998). When a fragile patient felt deeply hurt after spontaneous actions[14] on Fosshage's part, which he did not anticipate would affect her in this way, the patient was further disrupted by Fosshage's offer to share the reason for his actions on the basis that "illuminating her view of the uninterested other and offering an alternative perspective [would be useful]" (Fosshage, 1998, p. 134). The patient's response was: "Jim, when I come into the room, just check your subjectivity at the door" (ibid). Yet, after working through their rupture, which centrally entailed Fosshage's deep-going understanding of the patient's experience of being overwhelmed by his subjectivity, her cohesion was noticeably restored, and then she solicited—and apparently warmly welcomed—his telling her what led to his actions that precipitated her distress.

From the perspective of specificity theory, none of this could be predicted. One could not have anticipated that this patient would have been disrupted by the analyst's spontaneity. ("[Our] capacity to share humor often helped her to regain perspective") (ibid., p. 134). The application of the "theory" that sharing discrepancies between two "discrete" others, or that considering an other-centered perspective, like Fossshage's subjectivity, could be useful, turned out not to be so *in this case at this time.* Returning to the stance of empathically listening to the patient's in-depth experience of rupture of a selfobject mirror transference emerged as healing. This does not mean that the theory upon which the one response or the other is right or wrong. It means that in the specificity of process of a particular dyad, variegated "theory" may, or may not, emerge as useful. In practice, specificity theory would apprehend these sequences as constituting a process of creative discovery in which the analyst and patient must together *find out* what may make a therapeutic difference.

I attempted at one time to rationalize a guideline for sharing subjective experience based upon a structured theory. On the basis of self psychology theory, I supposed that a helpful guideline might be the relative cohesiveness, or not, of the patient's self. But this did not universally turn out to reflect my clinical experience. I have worked with vulnerable patients, apparently like Fosshage's, who have been in quite disrupted and even seriously fragmented states but for whom the sharing of my subjective feelings and thoughts has been crucially self-restoring; and I have worked with patients whose self was quite cohesive in context, for whom empathically fashioned mirroring was frequently an optimal, vitalizing response. I expect many of you have had similar experiences. The possibility of offering a response that is optimally therapeutic is enhanced when we stop relying upon the prescriptive application of structure theory and move to considering the efficacy of responsiveness based upon emerging dyadic discovery. Yet, should we jettison "theory" altogether, as in privileging the value of spontaneity?

Spontaneity and improvisation can be enormously effective (see Kindler, 2010; Ringstrom, 2001, 2010). Yet, it may not. Whether it is or not depends upon the specificity of process. I am reminded of a surprising experience during an analytic session with David, a young married architect with whom I always felt a comfortable, friendly sense of relatedness. When I spontaneously shared an experience of my own that was similar to the one he had just described, in which household decisions centered on the opinions of his wife, David exclaimed, with intense annoyance, "I thought this was about me!" I could not have anticipated this reaction from anything that was happening either in our prior verbal exchanges or on the basis of the prevailing ambience. With my spontaneous, "ordinary" response during our conversation (I hadn't even thought about it in terms of whether or not I should "self-disclose.") I uncovered my analysand's unconscious aversive experience to the situation that prevailed between himself, and his mother and his wife, and his need for something quite different, which I apprehended as a particular kind of selfobject *relationship* (Bacal, 1994). All this emerged in process in that moment; it was a discovery about me-and-him as reflecting his unconscious experience with his wife and his mother that he had ostensibly found "just fine." We also discovered, in effect, what was making a therapeutic difference to David—that I really listen to *him*.

Clinical experience has shown that sharing our subjectivity with our patients can, at times, powerfully move the therapy forward, yet at other times, it is not specifically helpful. But neither result is predictably useful on the basis of any priori perspective on responsiveness. Theory may emerge as useful in process, as self psychology theory variously appeared to, for me, in these examples.

Let's look a little more closely at the question of the analyst's transparency. Does the patient always "read" the analyst? It is perhaps true, as Miletic (1998) observes, that everything that an analyst does or says, or doesn't do or say, shows something about himself or herself (see also Renik, 1995). But is it also true, as he avows, that this is always registered by the patient? I have, for example, been dripping with sadness in sessions and my patient has clearly been quite unaware of this. While it is important to be alert to the possible effect of our unarticulated attitudes and affects, or the beneficial effect of declaring them, we cannot assume either that our patients always sense them or whether it is a good idea to share them. When we suspect that our patient may be picking up our subjectivity, would sharing this be therapeutic? If we believe that the patient likely discerns our feelings, and we hold to the theory that being transparent is therapeutic, not sharing our subjectivity—whether or not we also explore the patient's—would be a therapeutic error. If we hold to the theory that the emergence, unfolding, and deepening of transference is pivotal and would be interfered with by "disclosing," then sharing our subjectivity would be a therapeutic error, whether or not we believe the patient senses what we actually think and feel. Yet, any of these theories, or perhaps none of them, may hold water in the unpredictable specificity of unfolding process.

A subset of these questions is whether it is therapeutically optimal or not to answer the analysand's questions. Here is a brief vignette about "self-disclosure" in this context which illustrates that, when a therapist applies a particular theory to guide his responses, rather than allowing for the discovery of what may emerge as therapeutic in process (whether or not this may correspond to any "known" theory), she could find herself responding not so therapeutically. Some years ago, in an initial consultation, I was discussing with Barry, a young psychologist, about how I might be of help to him in analysis. At that time, I held a "theory" that the therapeutic ambience would be enhanced by answering questions, and that then enquiring about what motivated the question might be useful. As we talked, I felt comfortable answering questions Barry posed about how I worked, what my perspectives were on therapy, my policy about being available between sessions, and so on. Barry also seemed to be comfortable with our interaction.

During our second consultation, Barry told me that, when his former analyst answered questions, it tended to stop the process of his telling her more. For example, on one occasion, he told her that her dress looked sexy. When she responded to his question about whether she felt uncomfortable about his telling her this by saying she did not, for Barry their conversation seemed to stop there. Barry would have wished that his analyst had asked him how he felt about what he perceived, or how he felt about the analyst's not feeling uncomfortable about his sharing his observation with her. Another, apparently dynamically related interaction was Barry's experience of his analyst's response to a dream in which he felt that he pretty clearly depicted his analyst as a well-known male gay figure. In his associations to the dream, Barry wondered if this meant he thought his analyst was really gay. In an attempt to alleviate what Barry perceived as her assumption that if this were so, it would be particularly disturbing to him, the analyst responded that that she wasn't gay. Barry told me that he would have wished that she would have inquired how he felt about the possibility that his analyst was gay.

Interestingly, I discovered during our process that, for Barry, it was irrelevant whether or not his analyst would answer his questions or explore their meaning. Neither constituted what Barry felt he needed from his analyst, then, which was that she indicate a receptivity to receiving his feelings. Barry, implicitly referring to his experience of my earlier failure analogously to respond optimally, as well as to his hopes, added, "I want to be able to tell you *anything* about how I feel."

The important "questions" are, what is the patient looking for from the therapist, and from the therapy, and whether the analyst can respond optimally. If the analyst has a "set," in effect, a "theory" for example, that it is or is not therapeutic to be "anonymous," then he cannot discover, in process, what may be specifically therapeutic, then, for that patient. As we can see from this example, the question about anonymity may itself turn out to be spurious. For Barry, therapeutic priority was finding a particular kind of *therapist.* He appeared to be looking for a therapist who could sense and respond optimally to his great difficulty in sharing his feelings, but which he longed to do more than anything else. The way his current analyst—and I suspect, I too—appeared to him to be willing to reassure him by answering his questions conveyed to him that she, and I, would be prepared to share some of ours, but perhaps not inclined, or able, to discover the depth of his.

Analysts can appear somewhat uncertain or unclear about whether "guidelines" or "techniques" should be established for "self-disclosure." Lewis Aron and Owen Renik's approach to this issue is illustrative. Aron offers an exhaustive list with regard to when or what kind of self-disclosure may be offered (Aron, 1996, pp. 239–241), yet also cautions "[against replicating] Ferenczi's mistake of reacting against Freudian anonymity by going to the opposite extreme of self-disclosure as a standard technique. [It] should, instead, be viewed as one technical and personal option to be used with clinical discretion and mutual reflection . . . [however, it may become] too much a technique and lose some of the benefit that resides in its spontaneity and authenticity" (Aron, 1996, p. 239). That is, while Aron states "[his belief] that the question of the degree and nature of the analyst's deliberate self-revelation is open to resolution within the context of each unique psychoanalytic situation" (Aron, 1996, p. 253), he also alludes to the possibility of evolving a "theory of technique" that may "dictate" the analyst's decision about self-disclosure.

Renik believes it is important that we develop *"guidelines about what kinds of information about the analyst are useful to communicate to a patient"* (p. 468). Yet, Renik also conveys his appreciation of the specificity of responsiveness in an interesting vignette in which he responds differently to the same patient on different occasions, in the contexts of particular process at the time. "I reached a different conclusion about self-disclosure, based on my view of which of my thoughts were relevant to what my patient and I were collaboratively trying to understand about his mental life. In the first instance, I decided to state a perception of my own; and in the second instance, I decided not to state one" (p. 484).

Interestingly, though, in this case example Renik again offers this as another "technique" which is based on the structured theory that the patient always optimally experiences psychoanalytic treatment as a collaborative venture of equals. This sounds like it should be ubiquitously valid. But is this so? In that clinical situation, Renik felt he faced a "choice" with this patient with regard to confronting him about his ruminating but wonders whether he will be experienced as his disapproving father: he shares his dilemma with his patient. We would see this as a potentially useful sharing of his subjectivity that might emerge as therapeutic with a particular patient at a particular juncture—but as a universally applicable "technique"?

Specificity theory in effect responds to the challenge put forward by Renik (1995, p. 480) to offer "a systematic conception that can replace the principle of analytic anonymity" through its power in *not offering guidelines. In rejecting this position, it allows that responsiveness that may be of particular therapeutic value for the patient optimally emerge within the specificity of process of the particular dyad without structured preconceptions.*

From the perspective of specificity theory, it is not a matter of technique or guideline. There are no guidelines or techniques for "self-revelation" that are universally useful. Rather, the same considerations apply to the question of whether subjectivity should be shared that apply to any response: would it facilitate or impede that patient's therapeutic experience? And we can only "reliably" find out if we stop relying upon a priori assumptions of how we should be optimally responding, whether on the basis of apparently valid theory or upon the assumed superior yield of spontaneity. In the Fosshage example, spontaneity was disruptive and not therapeutic; with my patient, David, my spontaneous sharing created a temporary disruption, which usefully revealed a dissociated state of self-and-other.

The views of Orange and Stolorow regarding the sharing of the analyst's subjectivity are based upon intersubjective systems theory (Atwood, Stolorow, & Brandchaft, 1987). They see no "right answer" to questions about "self-disclosure" (Orange & Stolorow, 1998, p. 535). Nor do they regard it as a technical tool available to the analyst. Rather, they see "two people together, analyst and patient, trying to find understanding that will permit a reorganization of experience or perhaps a developmental second chance" (ibid.). This view is consonant with though not identical to the perspective of process specificity.

With specificity theory, what is central is the creative discovery by therapist and patient whether the sharing of the therapist's thoughts or feelings at that time may be useful or not in whatever way for that patient, and workable for that therapist. Such discovery optimally emerges within the particularity of process that develops between these two participants. From this point of view, the concept, "self-disclosure," should be retired.

NOTES

1. There are many more we may consider, which we hope to do at another time.

2. There have been exceptions to this. Some analysts—both classical and Kleinian—have considered psychotic conditions to be treatable through analysis.

3. For example, Hannah Segal (Segal, 1973) emphasizes that, with psychotic patients, rigorous adherence to the basic psychoanalytic method is necessary. "If the patient is to sort out what is external from what is internal, how far his world is colored by omnipotent phantasy, he can only do so if the analyst remains unaltered in his basic function" (p. 119). (That is, interpretation of primitive psychotic mechanisms that the patient utilizes to deal with these phantasies.)

4. Antipsychotic medication was instituted, but was of no use and in any case Dina was always very reluctant to take it.

5. I had the recollection, when working with Dina, of listening to Ronald Laing in London many years ago (personal communication, 1962) tell about how

he and his associates at Kingsley Hall were aided in their psychotherapeutic work with schizophrenics by taking 10 micrograms of the psychotomimetic, LSD. I am wondering, as I write this up, whether my reticence about saying to Dina that I did actually believe her delusions could, in part, conceivably have been a defense against moving to Dina in a way that unconsciously scared me—that is, the dread of resonating with her psychotic state.

6. The locked ward to which she was admitted at a prestigious teaching hospital locally was arguably a dismal and un-therapeutic place by any criteria.

7. Various formal definitions are offered by *The Edinburgh International Encyclopaedia of Psychoanalysis* (2006, pp. 462, 97); Charles Rycroft (1986, pp. 168–169, 25); Moore and Fine (1995, pp. 196, 47–48); Paula Heimann (1950), Joseph Sandler (1976); and James Fosshage (1994, 1995).

8. Interestingly, the more contemporary practice of defining both transference and countertransference as comprising all the feelings and attitudes of each participant toward the other actually extends their meaning beyond common usage—that is, the reactions of analyst and analysand to each other that may interfere with the progression of the treatment.

9. Sandler began as a classical analyst who moved to "object relations" theory late in his career and then became interested in Kohut's self psychology.

10. This is a subject I have addressed in some depth (Bacal, 1985, 1998; see also this book, pp. 48–50). It is also discussed by Ricci and Broucek (1998) who consider how this attitude may have derived from the anxiety on the part of the early psychoanalysts about public reaction to the sexual nature of psychoanalytic libido theory.

11. Renik (1995) conveys that analysts tend to avoid self-disclosure in order to cultivate their idealization, in effect to maintain an idealized, shame-free sense of themselves as different from the patient. As Stolorow and Atwood (1997) colorfully put it, we place a "cordon sanitaire" around ourselves (p. 339); then carefully regulate what we reveal. Yet, we may wonder to what extent this is generated within the specificity of process of the particular participants.

12. I initially defined "optimal responsiveness" (1985, p. 5) as the responsivity of the analyst that is therapeutically most relevant at any particular moment in the context of a particular patient and his illness."

13. Yet, it must also be recognized that self psychologists also have structured concepts that give substance to the therapeutic importance of offering a response as a discrete other who may respectfully oppose the patient's subjectivity: the adversarial selfobject relationship (Lachmann, 1986), or antagonistic selfobject relationship (Wolf, 1980); and Stolorow's self-delineating selfobject function (1992).

14. The patient had felt injured by Fosshage's apparent lack of interest in what she was saying by getting up in the middle of a session and adjusting the ventilation in the room; then made light of this with a humorously self-deprecating comment, "The mark of a good analyst—get up in the middle of a session and stare out the window" (Fosshage, 1998, p. 134).

9

Correlates of Specificity Theory within Infant Research

Louis Sander noted, in 2002, that a unity appeared to be emerging across ostensibly disparate scientific disciplines with regard to the complex components of life as process. Sander saw this as entailing the convergence of similar principles. I was fascinated to learn that, while I was exploring the specificity of process in psychoanalytic therapy and its implications for optimal therapeutic responsiveness (see Bacal, 1985, 1998), Sander and Tronick were elaborating their views about the significance of specificity for development and for therapy from within the discipline of infant research, and Gerald Edelman was developing a picture of the brain that in effect provided a neurobiologic substrate for all of it. Not long earlier, the philosopher, Hans Georg Gadamer (1975, 1979), following Heidegger, had put forward the view of understanding as constitutive in relation to the study of history. By this Gadamer meant that as we engage in the process of understanding another, we are inextricably a part of that understanding. The particularity of our engagement in the process of understanding contributes to and "constitutes" the understanding.

Sander's and Tronick's work on specificity was unknown to me until I came across their superb articles, "Thinking Differently: Principles of Process in Living Systems and the Specificity of Being Known" (Sander, 2002), and "Of Course All Relationships Are Unique: How Co-Creative Processes Generate Unique Mother-Infant and Patient-Therapist Relationships and Change Other Relationships" (Tronick, 2003). Many of their findings about specificity corroborate—and enrich—the perspectives of psychoanalytic specificity theory, which arose from my clinical experience with adult patients.

LOUIS W. SANDER

The conclusions that Sander draws from his infant research and its biological substrates in the concepts of Paul Weiss and Gerald Edelman strikingly correlate with the fundamental perspectives of specificity theory that we derive from the psychoanalytic situation. Sander (2002) considers specificity to be a fundamental principle of all human interaction. He refers to specificity in interaction and engagement as "recognition process." Sander understands "recognition process" as "the specificity of fittedness in therapeutic moments of recognition, in which a complex configuration of interactive elements . . . become well-enough aligned between patient and therapist at a specific point in time to open up new possibilities for what they can do together" (Sander, 2002 p. 40). "I propose this process as a bridge, at the human level, connecting basic principles of biological process with developmental process—through the negotiation of a sequence of increasingly complex tasks of adaptation, or 'fitting together,' between the infant and its caregiving environment over the first years of life" (2002, p. 13). He continues, "The principle of specificity of connection [is] required for the self-assembly of components into larger wholes at the level of awareness, [and] is basic to what we refer to as 'recognition process'—a process that brings two states of consciousness together in a moment of fittedness" (pp. 21–22).

Sander's infant research in effect affirms one of the fundamental perspectives of specificity theory we glean from psychoanalytic practice, that therapeutic process is centrally related to experiences of fit that are specific to a particular dyad. Specificity theory adds the concept of "optimal responsiveness" that aligns the therapist's contribution to the particularity of the patient's therapeutic need (see chapters 5–7, this book).

Sander appears to have initially derived his idea of specificity from the work of the biologist, Paul Weiss, who drew attention to specificity as "a principle, universally used in the living world." Weiss, using the dictionary meaning of *specific* as "having a special *determining* quality" (Sander 1995, p. 585), identified "the device of specificity" as a "chief biological device" that is critical in establishing and maintaining the connections upon which the coherence of living organization depends. "[This device] is essential for communication, recognition, affinity relations, and selectivity" (ibid.). Weiss, as early as 1970, described the basic principle as one of "'matched specificities'—a sort of resonance between two systems attuned to each other by corresponding properties . . ." (Sander, 2002 p. 19). Many of the case examples in this book depict how such resonant specificity is central to therapeutic effect.

Sander's views are also of particular interest to us as they concur with our view that the specificity of process in psychoanalytic therapy has a biologic substrate in Edelman's understanding of the development and functioning of the brain (see chapter 4, this book and Bacal & Carlton, 2008). As the brain interacts with its environment, which Edelman (1992, p. 81) calls "recognition," a specific response is selected (Edelman's "neuronal group selection," ibid., p. 83; see also chapter 4, this book). Edelman refers to the brain's function of continual adaptive matching, which constitutes a process of the fitting of elements in the organism to novelty occurring in the environment.

Sander regards Edelman's discovery of the intimate relationship between specificity in adaptive experiencing and the selection of neuronal group configurations as neurobiological analogue to his concept of recognition, or adaptive process, which is "an underlying principle of [psychological] development . . . in which specificity is central" (Sander, 1995, p. 587)

Some of Sander's examples of specificity-fittedness processes are compelling. One of them is depicted in a few minutes of film that his research team obtained. It centers on a father who is holding his newborn baby on his home lawn three days after his wife returned home from the hospital. The baby had become increasingly fussy, and the mother was unsuccessful in settling her. Apparently becoming embarrassed in the presence of the researchers, the mother gives the baby to the father, and goes into the house to bring out refreshments. Here is Sander's account of what happened (Sander, 2002, p. 20).

> The film shows the father standing on the lawn, holding the baby in his left arm, continuing to talk to the researcher, during which time the baby simply fell asleep and the two went on talking. Run at normal film speed of 30 frames per second, this is all one sees. Over the same few minutes, now run frame-by-frame, one sees the father glance down momentarily at the baby's face. Strangely enough, in the same frames, the infant looks up at the father's face. Then the infant's left arm, which had been hanging down over the father's left arm, begins to move upward. Miraculously, in the same frame, the father's right arm, which had been hanging down at his right side, begins to move upward. Frame by frame by frame, the baby's hand and the father's hand move upward simultaneously. Finally, just as they meet over the baby's tummy, the baby's left hand grasps the little finger of the father's right hand. At that moment, the infant's eyes close and she falls asleep, while father continues talking, apparently totally unaware of the little miracle of specificity in time, place, and movement that had taken place in his arms.

We expect Sander would concur with our view that when processes of specificity-fittedness are not functioning well, problems may occur with regard to therapeutic effectiveness, as well as with problems in development. We speak, in the vernacular, of the importance of "fit." We tend to regard the patients with whom we work well as those with whom we have a good "fit," yet we do not give this the attention it deserves. Patients with whom we have not been effective—perhaps especially those who do not undertake therapy after a consultation, or who may stop therapy, often with dysphoric affect and sometimes without being quite able to state why—may do so because such processes of specificity-fittedness are not operating well, or are hardly operating at all. While, as Bion observed (personal communication, 1967), a patient might take one look at you and never want to see you again, the analyst might struggle similarly.

Sander (2002, p. 33) conveys that processes of specificity are bi-directional in the interaction between infant to mother and mother to infant. He gives the example of how in one of his experiments, a mother's whole depressive demeanor and her attitude toward her infant changed dramatically when she discovered he could see and therefore could "know who is being good to him." This joins up with another fundamental perspective of specificity theory, that psychotherapeutic process ineluctably entails specific experience of reciprocal responsiveness between analyst and analysand (see chapter 7, this book).

Perhaps the most basic element in Sander's "thinking differently" (Sander, 2002, p. 35) is Sander's identifying uniqueness as a central principle in the organization of a living system, a principle that articulates with the essence of specificity theory. Both Sander's observations and our own intelligibly rest upon what Edelman regards as his most important finding: that every brain is unique (Edelman, personal communication, 2004; see also chapter 4, this book). For Sander, "dealing with ongoing processes in any given living system, [necessitates that we] . . . deal with the unavoidable actuality of uniqueness . . . Given the uniqueness of each us as individuals, in no two infant-caregiver systems will 'process' be alike . . ." (Sander, 2002, p. 35). The most basic tenet of specificity theory is that the *responsiveness* that determines therapeutic effect for a particular patient must centrally take into account the recognition of the *uniqueness* of *both* participants and how they creatively discover specifically therapeutic ways to be together.

Sander offers perspectives on psychotherapy that enable us also to consider the differences between his views and those of specificity theory. One of the major differences entails that which characterizes the distinction we draw between a relatively unalloyed process theory, such as specificity theory, and mixed models of process-and-structure theory. For example, Sander offers such a mixed model in according primary importance to the particular end point objective of experiencing a coherent and integrated sense of self (a structure concept) in his theory of the importance of specificity of interaction (a process perspective). While we would agree with the importance of such an objective, which is remarkably similar to that of Kohut's (1977) (see also D. H. Malan & P. Della Selva, 2006), specificity theory leaves open to discovery or co-creation by the participants in that particular dyad what constitutes therapeutic experience for that patient at that moment and over time as their particular process unfolds.

Sander also alludes to a mixed model of process and structure for psychotherapy when he observes, "How the experience of specificity of being known or recognized is conveyed obviously is at the heart of what the effective interpretation accomplishes—bringing therapist and patient into new 'moments of meeting'—the inclusiveness of new, expanded states of conscious connection" (2002, p. 39). Sander was, at that time, drawing attention to two factors that he regarded as intrinsic to therapeutic experience, along with *the* therapeutic act that promotes them, and a predetermined goal. The two factors intrinsic to therapeutic experience are "being known" and of "moments of meeting," the therapeutic act is interpretation, and the goal is "expanded states of conscious connection." The Boston Change Process Study Group, of which Sander is a member, offered a view (Stern et al., 1998) that therapeutic effect depended upon "something more than interpretation" (p. 903) namely, upon "moments of authentic meeting" (ibid.) that arise from "implicit relational knowing" (p. 904). Since then, the Boston Change Process Study Group has revised their view of the process entailed in therapeutic change. They (see Nahum, 2005) now recognize that psychoanalytic therapy is intrinsically "sloppy" (p. 693), that is, indeterminate and dyadically specific, a view that matches our perspectives (see also issue of *Psychoanalytic Inquiry*, 2010, Vol. 30:3). The views of the Boston Change Process Study Group and our own are especially similar insofar as we regard therapeutic interactions—including those that emerge "spontaneously" (see Kindler & Ringstrom, 2010; Fiscalini, 1994)—as highly specific to the process of the particular dyad.

Specificity theory does not consider any response a priori to be either special, or therapeutically essential. A salutary spontaneous engagement that an analytic couple co-creates will be only one of the many ways that optimal therapeutic process can unfold. Specificity theory also reminds us that, in the complex co-creative endeavor that we engage as psychoanalytic practitioners, each one us, together with our patient, must discover, in each moment and over time, what we are there for. In other words, we must find out, as our process unfolds, what constitutes "therapeusis" for any particular patient, and whether the reciprocal responsiveness that this entails is possible for our particular dyad.

KARLEN LYONS-RUTH

Lyons-Ruth, a colleague of Louis Sander, has explicitly applied his ideas to psychoanalytic therapy. Her views, expressed in Sander's language, interface with those of specificity theory in most respects. Their essential commonality is about the importance of fittedness as process unfolds, and about the way both conceive of it as being emergent, specific, creative and often non-verbal. Perhaps our main difference is with regard to certain emphases within such process. Lyons-Ruth conveys that within the possible commonality of overall goals, the local goals that occur along the way "are [improvisationally] constructed dyadically out of the encounters of the moment" (Lyons-Ruth, p. 92). While we would agree that this happens, and can happen effectively, we do not see process as always being only improvisational; we recognize the value of definitively utilizing concepts from formal structure theories that appear to emerge with therapeutic relevance, in process (this is particularly illustrated in this book in the vignettes in chapters 6, 7, and 8).

Lyons-Ruth emphasizes the purposeful ascertaining of joint goals; our emphasis is on the usefulness of discovery, and co-creation by the particular dyad of how the two participants might be together therapeutically at that time and over time. This fundamentally changes the way we work. Lyons-Ruth agrees with Sander that recurrent specificity of connection leads to vitalizing experience through the increase of coherence or wholeness that is thereby promoted within a dyadic system. Again, we enthusiastically allow that the latter can and does occur; but we emphasize the importance of discovery by the dyad of what their specificity of connection may optimally promote through a process of creative discovery that is unique to each therapeutic dyad. Vitalization, for instance, may or may not emerge as salient or central for that patient at that time. The same goes for the experience of "being known," which appears to constitute another, generalized "structure" perspective that Lyons-Ruth advances within the predominantly process-based concepts of Sander that Lyons-Ruth so beautifully applies to the psychotherapeutic venture (see Lyons-Ruth, 2000, pp. 92–94). While this, too, may emerge as central, even crucial, for a particular patient, we must keep in mind that, as valuable as this goal may be, like any other it may or may not be what that patient is looking for, and what that dyad can accomplish.

Lyons-Ruth refers to the Boston Change Process Study Group, and their early emphasis on the importance of "moments of meeting" (Stern et al., 1998, p. 903, 912). Specificity theory implies a way of working that also recognizes the value of procedural, or "implicit relational knowing" (p. 904–905), and consciously experienced "now moments" (910–912). Specificity theory, however, would not privilege any particular kind of response, interaction, or experience as constituting effective therapy. Specificity theory in effect asserts that when therapist and patient "meet," there are many different ways, implicit and explicit, that therapy may happen.

Lyons-Ruth describes in detail a process of interactive responsiveness between herself and a patient (Lyons-Ruth, 2000) that suggests she may recognize the importance of the reciprocal effect on each of them that influences their responses to each other. One of the central tenets of specificity theory, which is not prevalent in current theory of therapeutic action, is that responsiveness within any therapeutic dyad is *ineluctably* reciprocal—in various ways and to varying extents—with regard to psychological needs of the particular patient and those of the particular therapist in their interaction (see Bacal & Thomson, 1996, 1998, and pp. 80–81, this book). In other words, an important condition for a therapeutic process also entails a reciprocity of experience between patient and therapist that will be specifically workable for the two participants—a reciprocity that is unique, to that dyad. This, now, naturally leads us to consider the ideas of Edward Tronick, with which specificity theory has significant points of contact.

EDWARD Z. TRONICK

When my attention was drawn to Tronick's work (1998, 2003, 2005) after I had been developing specificity theory for several years, it came as a special and welcome surprise. Many of Tronick's findings and conclusions, which arise from infant research, are coincident with, and enrich, those of specificity theory, which arose from my psychoanalytic experience. Tronick draws attention to the uniqueness of relationship and its co-creation by the dyad. This uniqueness "emerges out of mutual regulatory recurrent *co-creative* interactive processes between the infant and another person . . ." (2003, p. 475). Tronick (1998, 2005) hypothesizes that a dyadic state of consciousness emerges when mutual regulation is especially successful due to the coordination of one individual's state of consciousness with the meanings of another's state of consciousness with respect to age-appropriate forms of meaning, and with regard to affects, relational intentions and representation.

Tronick explicitly distinguishes between "co-construction" and "co-creation" (2003, p. 475). The former implies a blueprint for getting to an end-state, while co-creativity implies neither. When individuals engage in mutual communication, their dynamics and direction are unknown, and how they will be together will only emerge from their mutual regulation. From this principle of co-creation, Tronick draws his "relationship differentiation hypothesis: relationships increasingly differentiate from one another over time. That is, relationships become more and more unique from one another over time as new forms of being together are co-created" (p. 476).

Tronick contrasts this view of the differentiation of relationships with those of RIGS, according to Stern or Model Scenes as described by Beebe and Lachmann that regard interactive regulatory patterns as abstract and depersonified ways of expecting to be with others. Relationships, according to Tronick, do not become increasingly decontextualized, that is, depersonified, they become increasingly personified and specific with regard to the individual. And, rather than become more ubiquitously relevant, they become progressively less transferable. One kind of unique implicit knowledge that develops within a mother-infant dyad is how the two participants are characteristically able to co-create and be together, in "time-activity-contexts," such as awakening, feeding, changing diapers, and playing. "The infant and the mother co-regulate an especially varied set of time activity contexts and they develop unique implicit knowledge of how they are together in each of these contexts." Tronick refers to this kind of uniqueness as "thickness" (pp. 478–479). Another kind of unique implicit knowledge on the part of infant and mother is knowing how they are able to work together to repair mismatches and disruptions, regardless of the content of the disruptions or of the particular moves in the relationship that generate them or repair them. Both the former—Tronick call this "metaprocedural" knowing—and the latter, the particular ways that the dyad interacts to do this, are *specific* to a particular relationship (p. 478). Yet, Tronick has observed that these ways may also vary: "[T]he infant's signal that worked one time may not work the next time, and the same is true for the caregiver's response, as most parents have experienced" (2005, p. 299). Tronick's observations on these varieties of unique interaction are reflected in the perspectives of specificity theory as applied to psychoanalytic process (see chapters 6 and 7, this book).

Tronick critiques the infant-centered perspective of the Boston Change Process Study Group and cautions that extrapolation from the infant-mother situation to the therapy situation should not be made without considering the differences in infant and adult emotional and cognitive capacities, states wherein they make sense of the world, and age-possible meanings over the course of development. He also holds, as does specificity theory, that in contrast to what the Boston Change Process Study Group has asserted, "not everything in adult therapy is the 'something more than insight process'" (2003, p. 485). The therapist and her adult patient have ways of being together that are qualitatively different from those of the infant, as well as from the child and adolescent. He reminds us that while infants may only live in the implicit, children and adults do not, that their states of consciousness include language, explicit knowing, different forms of representation, self regulation, analytic capacities, and much, much more . . . Words, symbols, representations and *insight* do count for adults." (ibid.) . . . "The conceptualization of co-creative regulatory processes suggests that there are many ways to induce change in therapy and that change can come through many domains" (p. 486).

Tronick's work articulates richly with the theoretical perspectives of specificity theory and the clinical approach it informs: that responsiveness which is optimally therapeutic within a particular dyad will be a function of how the particular participants can be with each other in the specificity of their interaction in the moment and over time.

In our final chapter, we consider how the perspectives of specificity theory can enhance the consultative, or "supervisory" process.

10

The Power of Specificity in the Process of Supervision

Discussing patient sessions with a "supervisor" is regarded as a centrally important aspect of training to become a psychotherapist.[1] The *Concise Oxford Dictionary* defines supervision as "[overseeing the] execution or performance of . . . [a person's] actions or work" (p. 1072), and Solnit (1970, p. 359) defines psychoanalytic supervision "as a process in which two or more people participate in a joint effort to establish, maintain, and/or elevate a level of performance." Today, many educators would agree with Ernest Wolf (1995) that the term, "supervision," is better regarded as *consultation* with a more experienced colleague; yet whatever we call it, we seem to have difficulty not only agreeing, but even clarifying, what it is optimally about.

Kindler (1998) observes that a good supervisor contributes in more diverse ways to the effectiveness of the treatment under supervision "[than through his] traditional roles of imparting technique, teaching theory, and formulating the psychodynamic meaning of the patient's communications" (p. 376). Yet, how many psychoanalytic educators even now would agree with Wolf that supervision constitutes a process in which learning depends upon the active participation of both participants in a mutually responsive relationship that entails "not only [sharing and creating] information . . . but simultaneously and necessarily also [sharing, creating, and participating] in each other's inner experience of themselves and of the other"? (Wolf, 1995, pp. 261–262). Wolf maintains that "[t]he purpose of so-called supervision is "[not only] to facilitate the emergence of . . . psychological skills and talents [but also] to strengthen . . . those personality traits that will enable the student-analyst to perform and to improve his psychoanalytic work" (p. 259). Yet, almost 40 years earlier, Michael Balint asserted that "the acquisition of therapeutic skill does not consist only of learning something new: it inevitably also entails a limited, though considerable, change in the [therapist's] personality (Balint, 1957, p. 299). More recently, Rosbrow (1997) described the teach-treat split as a false dichotomy based on the spurious premise that only interpretive work is legitimate in analysis and only instruction is appropriate in supervision.

Kindler (1998) has emphasized the importance of the supervisor's recognition that each analytic dyad is unique and, along with Fleming and Benedek (1966), that the newly established triad is mutually influenced by each of its members. Kantrowitz (2002a), on the basis of her research, arrives at analogous conclusions.

> The interaction of the characteristics of candidate, supervisor, and patient [affects] the candidate's learning and analytic work . . . The particular gains candidates derive from working with particular supervisors is a function of the specific needs arising from their stage of training, their previous experience, their character traits and conflicts, and their interaction with the character and conflicts of their patients. The complex nature of these interactional effects makes it increasingly apparent that no one model of supervision is applicable to all situations. (p. 966)

The application of specificity theory to supervision underscores the *uniqueness of each supervisory dyad and the emergent specificity of its process.* Its participants must address, in the particularity of *their* process, what constitutes optimal ways of teaching and learning, for them, with regard to the treatment of that patient, and what is possible for them to accomplish together.

Supervision is, in effect, a curious kind of hybrid that variously comprises teaching, training and, in some ways, treatment. Personal therapy may enable the student therapist to come to know himself better, help him to "change," and potentially increase his capacities as a clinician. He will, however, still encounter specific challenges as he engages with his patient in ways that may not be addressed—indeed, which may not arise—in that setting. Neither personal analysis nor traditional supervisory work reliably offers this specificity. The responses that an experienced supervisor may recommend to his supervisee will be helpful, only insofar as they may be useable by that student, and illuminate what may be therapeutically optimal, and workable, between her and her particular patient.

The back story to how psychoanalysts arrived at contemporary views on supervision comprises a tale of battling perspectives and, at times, confusion about just what supervision is or should be.

For some while, Freud and most of his early followers informally offered instruction to their analysands who were interested in practicing psychoanalysis. However, in 1935, it became apparent that in Bupapest, psychoanalysts had been doing it differently. As Alice Balint put it (A.

Balint, 1935), the character of the analyst figures significantly in the analytic situation. Balint's emphasis was on its potentially disturbing effect. A year later, Vilma Kovacs (1936), also an analyst in the Budapest Institute (and Alice Balint's mother) averred that "Further modifications of [the analyst's] technique and improvements in it are thus directly related to the analyst's personality . . . [The analyst must] constantly . . . observe the manifestations of his counter-transference, by which we mean his negative and positive affective attitude toward the patient" (Kovacs, p. 348).[2] Kovacs emphasized the importance of Freud's assertion, in 1910, "'that the pre-requisite for a successful application of psycho-analytical technique is that the physician should begin his analytical training by being analyzed himself'" (p. 348). Kovacs understood that Freud was asserting that it was only by knowing himself—especially his unconscious—that the analyst can recognize his patient's unconscious communications, and that it is essential for the success of the treatment that the analyst should analyze himself continuously. Years later, Isakower (1963) elaborated Freud's (1900) concept of the analyst or student analyst as an instrument of analysis (IJPA, 1970, 51, p. 358); and Grinberg suggested that "further self-analytic work" would also sharpen that instrument (see Solnit, 1970, p. 359). The view of the Budapest group was that the candidate's analyst, his "training analyst," should be doing the supervision, and that it was important that the student be in analysis while he was treating his patients (Kovacs, 1936). In effect, the Hungarian analysts were questioning how well that instrument could be honed by further analytic work unless self-understanding were concomitantly associated with consideration of the patient to whom it may apply.

At the "Four Countries Conferences" in the nineteen thirties, where European analysts met to present papers and to discuss problems,[3] it was agreed that in psychoanalytic training attention should be focused on two areas: the student's reactions to the patient's transference, and the teaching of analytic technique; and that more attention should be paid to the first of these than had hitherto been the case. To emphasize the difference between the two, the focus on the student-analyst's countertransference was termed "Kontrollanalyse," and the focus on teaching the student how to conduct analysis, i.e., "technique," was called, "Analysenkontrolle."[4] There was supposedly universal agreement about the nature of the latter and that it did not involve the student's countertransference. Yet, confusingly, the participants at the Four Countries Conferences also agreed that the two tasks of training "could not be divided" (Balint, 1948, p. 166). While it was not made clear just how this recommendation should be implemented, it seemed to imply that both the supervisor and the student's analyst were expected to address both areas. Interestingly, Kovacs had also reported (in 1936) that, in supervising candidates who were not in analysis—even those who had been in analysis with her but who presently were not—she had difficulty orienting herself adequately to the material in order to carry out her supervisory tasks: "I did not know the candidate's character and his modes of reaction, and so I could not say from what point of view he was judging the various situations he encountered" (Kovacs, 1936, p. 352). In her experience, "Analysenkontrolle" without "Kontrollanalyse" was superficial and unsatisfactory; that is, she felt that she could not adequately supervise someone that she did not know.

Alice Balint and Michael Balint (1939) described the great variation in so many of the supposedly universal ways that analysts work, which reflected their "personal" (p. 224), i.e., individual preferences. This suggested that despite efforts to adhere to Freud's technical recommendations, "analytic technique" was far from universally the same. It also implied that in "teaching" candidates "how to" conduct an analysis, we should not ignore an omnipresent variable: who the analyst is. The Balints also asserted—preceding by almost 50 years the elaboration of intersubjectivity theory by Stolorow, Brandchaft, and Atwood (1987)—that "the analytical situation is the result of an interplay between the patient's transference and the analyst's countertransference, complicated by the reactions released in each by the other's transference on to him" (p. 227).

The earliest, and most famous, proponent of "teaching" the student was Max Eitingon, one of Freud's early followers. Eitingon felt that characteristic inadequacies and learning problems of the beginner required that he be taught the technique of psychoanalysis. When the student is confronted with a patient, his "so-called completed analysis" is not the only experience that leaves him "helpless." Eitingon maintained that it was "necessary to teach the technique of psychoanalysis through another method . . ." (Fleming & Benedek, 1966, p. 11). In contrast to Kovacs, Eitingon was certain that the supervising analyst could, and should draw attention to characteristic beginner's mistakes "even if he had not known the candidate through working with him" (ibid., p. 11).

The participants at successive Four Countries Conferences agreed that both personal analysis and supervision were essential to psychoanalytic training. However, while most participants seemed to agree that the analysis of the countertransference was the most important part of the training,[5] unclarity prevailed with regard to the setting in which this should take place. And no decision was made about whether the training analyst or someone else should begin supervising the candidate. Eventually it was agreed that further experience was needed before this could be decided. However, in 1947, apparently without further research or discussion, the "London Standing Rules" (according to Balint, Ernest Jones's rules) were proclaimed: "The analyst undertaking the student's personal analysis does not undertake the supervision of his cases" (Balint, 1948, p. 165).[6]

At that point, a pedagogic "big bang" occurred within the psychoanalytic universe. The "tripartite" system of analytic training officially came into being, with the strict separation of its three modalities: the psychoanalysis of the candidate, the treatment of cases under supervision, and theoretical lectures and seminars. Training programs for dynamic psychotherapy variously included all three. They emphasized the central importance of supervision, with therapy as an option if the student's personal problems seemed to be getting in the way of his clinical work.

In Hungary, this did not happen. Balint (1948) explicitly stated the view of the Hungarian institute that the candidate's clinical training can be best done if the personal analysis and the supervision are carried out by the same person, that is, the candidate's analyst, at least with the first case. In other words, the optimal situation for "supervising" the candidate, according to the analysts in the Budapest Institute, is the one in which the supervisor may address personal problems in depth that affected his work with his patient. While Ferenczi did not explicitly participate in this declaration, one can see his "mark" on these perspectives.

Balint, who had been trained by Ferenczi, emigrated to England in 1939 from Hungary, where he had been director of the Budapest Psychoanalytic Institute. The British Institute permitted Balint to practice the Hungarian analysts' approach to supervision for the candidate analysand's first case, providing he offered this on a voluntary basis. If the candidate chose to opt for this, he was required by the Institute to treat an additional control case under the supervision of another training analyst. I have described my experience of this method of supervision in chapter 2. Essentially, it entailed the spontaneous discussion of his experience with his patient during the analytic hour.

As far as I know, every psychoanalytic training organization (and those offering training for psychodynamic psychotherapy), apart from the institute in Budapest, complied with Jones's edict. The "training" analyst just analyzed the candidate, and the supervisor just taught him "how to do analysis." Yet, while everyone except the Hungarians seemed to welcome this arrangement, the appearance in the literature of many papers in which analysts continued to debate what constitutes optimal supervision suggested that the controversy that began in the mid 1930s which supposedly ended with the implementation of the "London Rules" had not cooled down all that much. It also implied that the implementation of these rules may not have delivered the educational yield that Jones and his faithful followers assumed it would.

In the early 1950s, at the Tavistock Clinic in London, Michael Balint and his wife, Enid, also a psychoanalyst (Alice tragically died of a ruptured aneurysm shortly after she and Michael emigrated to England) developed another application of the Hungarian approach to psychoanalytic supervision.[7] They trained psychoanalysts to lead discussion groups (which later came to be called "Balint Groups") for general practitioners, psychiatric social workers, clergy, and probation officers in which the effectiveness of psychoanalytic ways of listening and responding were explored in those settings (Balint, M. 1957; Balint, M. & E., 1961). The identification of how individual characteristics of the doctor, social worker, etc. affected the therapeutic process was regarded as central; and the group's leader addressed this at different levels of recognition, depending largely upon the way the particular group leader functioned (see Gosling, Miller, Turquet, & Woodhouse 1967).[8] My own experience conducting these groups at the Tavistock Clinic, between 1961 and 1970 (Bacal, 1972, 1975a, 1975b) was also significant in alerting me both to the "treatment" aspect of this training and to the specificity of effective therapeutic interaction.

Michael Balint died in 1970, and I had not been in touch with Enid since I left London in 1971. I recently learned that she had written a book with members of a research group, to consider developments in the psychological aspects of general practice since Michael first elaborated his ideas. Both the group's way of working and what they discovered about the doctors' capacities for therapeutic work demonstrate remarkable points of contact with our views about the uniqueness and specificity of pedagogic, as well as therapeutic, process.

> [Our aim was] to have a wider look at the . . . uncertainties which abound in working with patients; while at the same time not attempting to reduce them to neat patterns, leaving the perspectives as wide as possible in the realization that what one person sees from one angle cannot be seen from another's . . . the doctors [came to] realize that their healing powers were strictly limited, but . . . on the other hand, observed that very small changes in a person can produce amazingly large effects on the life of an individual. It seems that the unique relationship which occurs in the general practice setting informs us as to what the work is really about. (E. Balint et al., 1993, pp. 98–99)

Four main themes have emerged in the psychoanalytic literature about supervision. These themes in effect address and elaborate the same issues debated by the attendees at the Four Countries Conferences in the 1930s. They essentially comprise the following questions: (1) Should the supervisor primarily be "teaching" the supervisee how to conduct a psychoanalysis, explicitly focusing on principles of analytic conduct and, implicitly—and inevitably—emphasizing the relevance of particular analytic theory? (2) Should the focus of supervision primarily be on the supervisee's patient or on the supervisee and his characteristic problems? (3) Should the focus be on process—between the supervisee and his patient, or/and between the supervisor and the supervisee; and (4) In what ways and how personally should the supervisor engage the supervisee in addressing "transference-countertransference," or "relational," issues, either between her and her patient or/and between her and the supervisor?

Despite the recognition by many analysts that "supervision is more than education and less than treatment" (Solnit, p. 359), there has been little in the psychoanalytic literature about the Hungarian method of analytic supervision since Balint's paper of 1948,[9] that is, on the role that the candidate's analyst might play in "supervision." This kind of supervision, in which the candidate's analyst may respond to her analysand's spontaneous discussion of her clinical experience, offers a potentially useful form of "education-cum-therapy." It would be especially useful in addressing specifically significant aspects of analytic process.

Some contributions to the literature do, however, suggest the influence of the Hungarian analysts' perspectives. In his presentation to the Third Pre-Congress on Psychoanalytic Training, Solnit (1970) also reported that "Although there [was] general agreement that the resolution of countertransference was the task of the student's own analysis, most institutes expect the supervisor to take it up tactfully and to deal with its educational implications if that is feasible" (p. 359). Pulver's (1984) view is that the ongoing debate as to whether supervision "should be considered purely an educational experience or whether it should, in addition, be therapeutic" is spurious; he concludes that "the question . . . can be answered solely from the dynamics of the supervisory situation" (p. 489). Pulver "[disagrees] with Keiser (1969) that [Fleming and Benedek] are much too therapeutic in their approach" (p. 490). He conveys that what may be identified as therapeutic work for the supervisee can be very useful for his analytic work with his patient (see also Levy & Parnell [2001]). Pulver concurs with Ekstein and Wallerstein that it is the purpose to which the supervisor's responses are put that render them appropriate. For Pulver, "[Supervision] is a powerful interaction, filled with emotions and made even more complex by the fact that it is an interaction about an interaction" (Pulver, 1984, p. 489). Interestingly, Pulver believes it is useful to "teach" analytic students not only about transference, resistance, and interpretation, but also, like Freud, Isakower, and others, to emphasize the importance of self analysis.

Dewald (1981), anticipating Kantrowitz's findings, draws attention to the importance of the supervisor's "[making] an assessment of the candidate's needs and vulnerabilities . . . as a guide for interventions" (p. 80). He wonders "[whether] the student [should] be expected to adapt his/her learning process to the supervisor's teaching methods and style [or whether] the supervisor [should] be expected to adapt his/her teaching methods and activity to the learning needs and limitations of the students?" (p. 85). Reflecting upon how "unsettled" (ibid., p. 85) this question has continued to be, Dewald considers that it "cannot be resolved in a uniform way, but . . . must be given consideration by each supervisor" (ibid.). Specificity theory concurs with this, but adds a further perspective: *consideration of the specificities of possibility within the process of any particular supervisory dyad.*

Fleming and Benedek (1966) recognize the usefulness of a systems, or process, approach in supervision. They regard supervision as "an experience where the teacher who is also an analyst can use his system-sensitivity and system-responsiveness, and his self-analytic function as flexibly for teaching as for analyzing, recognizing the different goals in each experience" (pp. 237–238). In their study of supervision transcripts, the goal of teaching the students about *process* was common to all supervisory activity. Their view is that "(t)eaching the student to regard psychoanalysis as a process is the most important and probably the most difficult of the supervisory tasks" (p. 53). I have indeed found that when offering case examples in clinical seminars and at analytic conferences for discussion of the specificity of psychoanalytic process, participants tend to wander away from a focus on process to talk about the psychodynamics of the case based on one theory or another and how the analyst might on that basis effectively intervene. Interestingly, in his otherwise commendatory review of Fleming and Benedek's book, Pulver (1984, p. 491) comments that it is "flawed" because they "devote at least a chapter to systems theory . . . in an attempt to lend to the study a theoretical background acceptable to science"(!).

We agree with Fleming and Benedek that a systems sensibility is crucial to effective supervision. Fleming and Benedek regard "[s]upervisory work [as requiring] an even greater span of system sensitivity than is necessary for analytic treatment . . . The supervisor [must be] [attuned to the patient and the analyst, the relationship between them and to the progress of the analytic process, [as well as to the relationship between the student and the supervisor]" (p. 56).

Fleming and Benedek come closest to articulating our view of the uniqueness of dyadic process and its specificity in supervision. "What the student learns in one supervisory session about his patient and/or about himself, he can apply only in the future to situations which are similar but never identical . . . The 'experience' itself can never be repeated" (p. 238). Specificity theory regards the supervisory situation as a process that is constituted by the emergence of dyadic specificities in at least the two situations of supervisor and supervisee, and supervisee and his patient, each of which may reciprocally affect one another. Other dyads—the student analyst and his analyst, the supervisor and the student's analyst—as well as the adjacent systems of the training institute and its "training committee," or "student progress" committee, may implicitly, sometimes also explicitly, come into play. Ultimately, the dyad comprising supervisor and supervisee, variously affected by these adjacent systems, will discover, within the specificity of their process, what constitutes possibilities for optimally responsive "supervisory" work for the particular candidate's educational needs. What that student needs, and what he or she can use from that supervisor at that time, and how this matches the supervisor's views and capabilities, will unfold within their unique pedagogic process. Supervisee and supervisor must learn together how they can optimally learn, work and, as Aronson (2000) suggests, play together.

Aronson (2000) offers a Winnicottian perspective on supervision that very much matches ours. He characterizes an optimal supervisory process as a "playful, creative experience . . . [a] 'to and fro,' in which . . . each participant [places] his particular stamp on the material and process, creating an exchange of sorts. In essence, the supervisee develops the capacity to discover—himself, the patient, the process of psychoanalysis—while concurrently allowing himself to be found by the patient, by himself, and by the supervisor" (p. 125).

Yet, somewhat surprisingly, Fleming and Benedek at one point add that "In the supervisory situation, the student goes back and forth between his knowledge of *how it should be done* (my emphasis) and what he actually did" (ibid., p. 32); and they "[emphasize] the importance of the teacher's awareness of *what he wants the student to become*" (my emphasis) (p. 235). In other words, someone really knows—and then at some point, the student also knows—just the way it should be done, how a well-trained analyst should practice (!) Morton and Estelle Shane (1995) effectively question this value in their article critiquing the constraints imposed by the American Psychoanalytic Association upon analytic candidates in the write-ups of their supervised cases. The Shanes make a "plea for flexibility and contextual understanding in the application of standards . . . that they be broadened in a way that reflects current analytic practice and individual analytic process" (p. 238).

Specificity theory does not pre-empt how it "should" be done, or "can" be done, nor what kind of analyst that student should become. Rather, the supervisor and supervisee will optimally "teach" each other by becoming aware of what the supervisee's learning needs are at that time, in relation to that patient, as they become specifically evident, either in the process between her and her patient or/and between her and the supervisor. Intrinsic to specificity theory is its emphasis on uniqueness, unpredictability and the specificity of process. While the supervisor will inevitably—and *perhaps* usefully—have in mind, consciously or unconsciously, what it means to work in the "right" way as a psychoanalyst, specificity theory allows that neither the supervisor nor the supervisee knows in advance the best way for the supervisor to teach that student, or how or what he or she should learn. They can, however, discover this—and how effectively this can be carried out within that supervisory dyad, through the specificity of their unfolding process. In effect, any or all of the four ways described (above, pp. 132–33) may variously emerge as *specifically* relevant in process.

In the Budapest approach to analytic supervision, where the supervision of the student-analyst's case takes place during his own analytic sessions,[10] these various ways of "teaching" are undertaken against the backdrop of the in depth recognition of who the student-analyst is, and what he now struggles with, in relation to that patient. While this method is not formally recognized in any of the three analytic institutes where I supervise candidates, I offer it informally in two ways. With my trainee analysands in analysis, I respond to their wish for help with their patients, while keeping my sensibilities open to how our interacting in this way affects my analysand and myself and our analytic work. Her analytic work with her analysand is a part of who *she* is, which comprises one of the strivings and goals for *her* life. With my awareness, in addition, that our commonly shared outside system—our training institute—apparently regards our analytic work as central to his *her* development as an analyst, I believe it would be remiss of me not to respond as helpfully as I can, within this context. The alternatives of "just listening," or interpreting associations about the patient only as they may personally relate to her, or suggesting she take the problem she is having with her patient to her supervisor fall just as short as the traditional recommendation of the supervisor that the supervisee take her "countertransference" problem up with her analyst.

My way of working with supervisees has significantly changed under the influence of specificity theory. I am much more aware of the variability and specificity of what the particular supervisory pair, of which I am one of the participants, can or cannot do together. When there is a good fit between myself and my supervisee, we can work well together. It is useful to be aware when the fit within this educational dyad may be less than optimal. Apprehending the nature of the particular limitations we face as a supervisory couple enables us to discover more clearly what we *can* do together, perhaps even find ways that we may "exceed expectations." In some current settings in which I supervise, I have found more latitude to work in this way because of the ethos of openness about sharing personal experience as it may affect analytic work.

Despite their recognition of the value of the Hungarian method of supervision, Ekstein and Wallerstein (1958) remain concerned to clarify the difference between training and treatment. For them, the main difference between the two is one of purpose which, they imply, can become muddled in the way the Budapest analysts worked. They emphasize that the purpose of supervision is educational. Its aim is "leading [the student] toward greater skill in his work with his patients" (p. 254). Yet they recognize that supervision is "[not] simply a didactic experience in which a body of knowledge is transmitted," and they appear to appreciate the value of not making the delineation between teaching and treatment too sharp.

> [S]upervision—that is, the supervisory process—[is] not simply . . . the transmission of knowledge and skills, but rather . . . a complex process that goes on between the supervisor and his student. This process is a helping process in which the student is being helped to discover his problems as a psychotherapist, to resolve them with the help of the supervisor . . . This process includes affective problems, interpersonal conflicts, problems in being helped, as well as in helping, and is truly itself a helping process. (p. 251)

This qualification brings their perspective on supervision closer to that of Balint, who viewed "the acquisition of therapeutic skill [as consisting not] only of learning something new but "inevitably also [entailing] a limited, though considerable, change in the [therapist's] personality" (Balint, 1957, p. 299). The point, it seems to me, that Ekstein and Wallerstein effectively make, is the one that specificity theory expressly addresses: that the challenges that any particular educational dyad face could be any of the ones they describe, or any combination of these. Ekstein and Wallerstein regard supervision as a *process*. Specificity theory adds that intrinsic to such a process is that it will be both specific for that particular supervisee, as well as possible for that particular supervisor.

I will illustrate with two examples how the perspectives of specificity theory influence the supervisory process. The first example is my précis of a supervision described by Ekstein and Wallerstein (1958), which demonstrates the implicit use of what we identify as the specificity of process. The second is a description of how one of my supervisees and I worked together.

Illustration 1

Dr. L, a beginning analytic candidate who was already an experienced psychotherapist, had just completed her personal analysis, and was working with her first control case under the supervision of Dr. James. Dr. L's patient was described as woman who had a restricted, inhibited, "hysterical" personality, who suffered from "hysterical vomiting" (p. 257), and utilized phobic arrangements to avoid situations that might evoke her symptoms. Dr. L frequently reported her concern to Dr. James that her patient made no reference at all to her, that she showed no sign of "transference feelings." Dr. L noted, too, that the patient did not refer to any feelings when talking about her aunt, who had played a substantial part in her upbringing. It was apparent to the supervisor that the analyst was immensely important "for this particular patient" (p. 257) and that the analysand was avoiding awareness of this in order to preclude experiencing her symptoms in relation to her analyst. The analyst did not move to interpret this, however. She had begun to feel that perhaps the patient was right. That is, although she was aware of the dynamics of transference, she was experiencing the patient's behavior as a true reflection of herself. It was hard for her to see herself as being so important to another person, and she also wondered whether she might be afraid to be apprehended in this way, from an archaic place within the patient.

In discussing the situation, Ekstein and Wallerstein consider that the student's experience could be viewed as a countertransference reaction, and that the feelings evoked in the analyst reflected issues that had not been resolved in her analysis; and that one way of responding would be for the supervisor to recommend that she return for more analysis. An alternative view, they suggest, would be that the student hadn't yet substantially apprehended the vicissitudes of transference, and that she needed more instruction about how to conduct analysis. The former view "would correspond to the early conviction in psychoanalytic training that the personal analysis really was the essential preparation for the future analyst. The second solution would correspond to the notion that supervision ought to consist only of the giving of technical information in a didactic form" (p. 258). So how should the supervisor respond?

Ekstein and Wallerstein recognize that supervisors have particular predilections and preferences for how they supervise, partly as an expression of their personalities. Some supervisors feel comfortable discussing countertransference issues with their supervisees at a personal level and interacting with them around these issues as they emerge, either in relation to the patient or/and in relation to themselves. Some supervisors do not, however, and prefer to address them in general terms, or only didactically, or not at all, and may refer the student back to her analyst for more personal analysis.

Dr. James learned that Dr. L was not only aware of the dynamics of transference, she also understood the patient's defensive need to avoid becoming affectively involved with her. She could also see that she was acting in accordance with the patient's "indirect command" that she stay away. However, she "did so because she felt paralyzed by a feeling that, in spite of it all, the patient was perhaps correct in her estimate of the analyst" (p. 259).

Dr. L's supervisor addressed the discrepancy between the lack of his supervisee's therapeutic action and her actual insight into the total situation, and then wondered whether it might derive from her own self-depreciatory inclinations. He learned from Dr. L that her tendency to depreciate herself was a problem that she had successfully addressed in her analysis in the context of her private life, but which seemed to resurface in work situations where she "could learn only when her respect for the teacher went hand in hand with self-depreciating attitudes" (p. 259). That is, Dr. L and Dr. James came to recognize that her "pseudo-ineffectiveness" (ibid.) with her patient was specifically associated with an accommodative attitude toward Dr. James, which she enacted with her patient. As this was understood, her work became more spontaneous and effective with this patient.

Three dimensions of this situation stand out: (1) The specific problem that emerged for the analyst, experientially, in relation to her patient was the same problem as the one that appeared to be unconsciously operating in relation to her supervisor; (2) The problem the trainee had in treating her patient was apparently resolved following an inquiry by the supervisor about a personal issue—a problem in maintaining her sense of her efficacy under certain conditions; and (3) Its resolution occurred in the context of exploring these conditions as they occurred in her relationship with her supervisor. That is, Dr. L's problems in being therapeutically effective with her patient could be understood and were resolved through the process of addressing a particular way that she experienced the relationship with her supervisor, and how this played out, apparently in displacement, in relation to this patient.

This supervisee was new to analytic work, but it was not teaching of "technique" that she needed, nor analysis, but rather *the addressing of a particular dimension of relational specificity* with her supervisor, which reflected a problem personal to herself, that emerged in relation to him and was also apparent with her patient. We could suppose that, regardless of how well her analysis might have gone, this problem may not have been adequately dealt with, or, like many issues that are "dealt with" in analysis, it may re-emerge under the stress of particular circumstances. What transpired in Dr. James's work with Dr. L depicts the implicit application of specificity theory in supervision; that is, a process approach that is useable by that particular supervisee and—although in this example only implicitly indicated—possible for that particular supervisor.[11]

While the purpose of the supervision was maintained—to improve the analytic skills of the trainee—the way in which this happened for Dr. L with Dr. James was through addressing the *specificity of process*, in this case, between the supervisor and the supervisee, that had its counterpart in the setting of the analyst's work with her patient. Perhaps there is a certain kind of "training" implicit in this way of working. We might call this "process training" which, in effect, Fleming and Benedek recommend (1966). Some would regard this as an example of "parallel process," a concept that we will consider from the perspective of specificity theory later in the chapter.

Ekstein and Wallerstein express the hope that supervisors "could make choices . . . which derive from the specific problems and needs of the learner rather than from their personal preferences and their personal security as teachers" (1958, p. 261). While I resonate with their "hope," I think that the way we could most usefully approach this challenge is by training supervisors to recognize the possibilities and limitations of the particular dyad of that supervisor with that supervisee as they emerge in process, just as we recognize this with regard to the specificity of the process between the trainee-analyst and her patient; and then try to discover how *their* process can be enhanced.

In an early attempt to assess the ingredients of effective training in Balint groups, (Bacal, 1971), I reported what seemed to constitute the "limited though considerable change" in the doctor to which Balint had referred (Balint, 1957, p. 299). Two factors emerged as pivotal: (1) that the doctor engage in work commensurate with his limits and makes appropriate use of consultant help; and (2) the interference by his own psychopathology in his work is minimal (Bacal, 1971, p. 13). Reasonable—and fairly obvious—criteria. What is also "obvious," though insufficiently observed, is what I learned over the next 40 years—that what must be added to these factors is the specificity of such an educational process. Its effectiveness will have a good deal to do with the exploration by educator and student within their process as to how they can best work together—or if they can at all.

Notwithstanding the knowledge we have acquired about clinical theory and how to apply it usefully, we all are, in a sense, beginners, with every patient. We learn anew—as we listen to each one of them and, simultaneously to ourselves—how we may or may not be able to respond therapeutically. As supervisors, we must also listen anew to each particular supervisee, and simultaneously to ourselves to discover how we may be helpful to him or her. What the discussions in the literature on supervision miss—and what was unnoted even by the Hungarian school—is that this kind of supervisory work usefully focuses not only on the "neurotic" or "characterological" issues of the "analytic instrument" that were impeding the treatment[12] but also upon the vicissitudes of what is specific, for good and ill, of the particular dyad as they become apparent, with regard to the treatment of that patient. The candidate's particular predilections as well as his "pathology" will emerge, for better or worse, in the specificity of process with his analysand or/and with his "training analyst." That is, what the analysts in Budapest did not quite recognize was that they had stumbled upon a *new* dimension of training—attending to the specificity of process of that trainee-analysand with his particular patient as it appears to emerge in that setting as well as in that of his "personal" analysis.

This brings us to a consideration of the idea of "parallel process" and whether it may usefully articulate with the concept of specificity of process.

SPECIFICITY AND "PARALLEL PROCESS"

The concept of parallel process, first introduced by Searles in 1955, has been applied extensively in supervision (see especially Ekstein & Wallerstein, 1958, pp. 177–196). Parallel process is generally regarded as evoked replication within the supervisory situation of unformulated and/or unaddressed difficulties variously experienced by the candidate within his relationship with his patient or/and within the supervisee's own personal analysis.

Opinion about the determinants of the phenomenon and its value differ considerably. Lesser (1983) even questions its existence, calling it an illusion. Rosbrow (1997) questions the value of the concept because drawing attention to its expression as a basis for understanding the difficulties the supervisee is having with his patient places the supervisor in a position of unquestioned authority about what is going on and may unnecessarily embarrass or even humiliate the student. Yet, as Baudry (1993) suggests, parallel process may constitute enactments in supervision of identifications based on unconscious shared anxieties or defenses by analyst and patient which may have important communicative value and could lead to valuable insight "if exploited with sensitivity by the supervisor" (p. 606).

Miller and Twomey (1999) challenge the merit of the parallel process concept on the basis of their view that "in each dyad there is a unique relational experience . . . shaped by each person's experience of self and other . . . It would seem unlikely that such a relational configuration and its dynamics would be so replicated within another equally unique dyad as to offer the kind of specific understandings that would prove clinically illuminating" (1999, pp. 576–577).

Yet, it is just this "replication" that, paradoxically, informs Grey and Fiscalini's (1987) view of parallel process as representing a "*complexity*" . . . a series of interlocking transference-countertransferences; that is, reciprocal neurotic integrations, which are linked by the participants' attraction to the same mode of defensive relatedness . . . In parallel process, as in life generally, people behave the way they do because this is the way they are, at least under the given circumstances" (p. 140). Doerman (1979) and Gediman and Wolkenfeld (1980) regard parallel process as entailing a complex multidirectional system of patient, therapist, and supervisor.

THE SPECIFICITY OF FIT AND THE SUPERVISORY PROCESS

These perspectives on parallel process suggest that it may arise as a result of the emergence of specificity-fittedness within the process of a particular psychoanalytic dyad or from unconscious resistance to experiencing this. Interestingly, the case examples of parallel process that Ekstein and Wallerstein offer illustrate only unidirectionally operating issues arising from the therapist-patient system, although they suggest that "[the] parallelism can work in reverse as well" (p. 196). Their fleeting recognition of the latter accords with Gediman and Wolkenfeld's observation of how, in a supervision group whose members comprised senior analysts, "parallel reenactments emerged relentlessly" (p. 251), and where the groups often disbanded because of the reluctance of the participants to openly present their work.

I have wondered whether the traditional arrangement of separating the modalities of "training" and "treatment" are in some measure responsible for the phenomenon of parallel process. Why does the student therapist bring to supervision an unconsciously disguised representation of the problem with his patient, yet one that is curiously revealing to the supervisor or, as characteristically happens, to a supervisory group? Could this possibly be because he is unconsciously, though ambivalently and "resistively," seeking help with a specific problem in relation to his patient that feels "personal" and similar, a problem that his therapist may not have responded to, but with which he does not anticipate adequate help, either, from the supervisor, in that setting?

From the perspective of specificity theory, recognizing and attending to the possible effect of one system operating on another, how in particular supervisory situations specific issues that remain unaddressed in other systems may play out, can be productive. Sometimes the parallel is "seen" at the outset, sometimes not. In my experience, especially in experiential supervisory groups (and in particular, where group therapists discuss their experience in their own groups), this can be a useful teaching tool. The important consideration is whether and, if so how, the particular supervisee and that supervisor, or supervisees, can deal effectively with them.

We do not give enough consideration to the importance of "fit" between particular supervisors and particular supervisees. I have worked with supervisees with whom the fit or lack thereof made a considerable difference to what we could do together. In some classically oriented institutes, the candidate's supervisor is still selected for her. And I have been witness to the disgraceful occurrence of the censuring of a candidate in one of these Institutes when she decided to leave her supervisor for another one.

Aronson (2000) writes trenchantly about his experience with three different supervisors whose quite different responsiveness to him and to his work with his patient resulted in quite different experiences of fit and concomitantly of the usefulness of the supervision. With Supervisor A, Aronson presented his work, and Dr. A found fault in it. "We often clashed over what was occurring both in the treatment and between us." Although "Dr. A was quite on the money with some of the observations about me and the patient . . . the tone that characterized our supervisory sessions made it impossible for me to truly take in the valuable things Dr. A. had to offer . . . I also began to feel that the true nature of my work was not being represented, and that an emergence of who I truly was as an analyst was being stifled" (p. 127). Aronson found Supervisor B much more helpful. "I came to realize how I was different and yet the same with patients [who were, in so many ways, very different], which, to me, resulted from our 'to and fro' exchanges and represented true use of the potential space . . . our supervisory sessions were characterized by humor and warmth" (p. 128). Aronson also learned a great deal from Supervisor C, who "had a quiet style and allowed me, even encouraged me, to work analytically" with the often quite disturbed youths in his practice (p. 129). He knew beforehand that former supervisees extolled Dr. C's supervisory work and his sensitivity to children. So he expected a good experience with him; but he was surprised to learn that other students who had been in supervision with him not only based their work on a wide range of theoretical orientations, but spoke of their more active, directive therapies that they presented to Dr. C, some of which sounded very much like cognitive-behavioral therapy. Dr. C was apparently able to work with these supervisees in the way that was most comfortable for each of them, even though it was at variance with his own personal style and preferences.

The importance of the specificity of fit within the supervisory situation is richly documented by Judy Kantrowitz (2002a, 2002b). Kantrowitz's research indicates that a propitious fit between candidate, supervisor, and patient can aid professional and personal analytic development and that a clash or enmeshment can impede it.[13] The candidates whose work she studied volunteered to discuss their experience of particular triadic matches "because they believed they illustrated a particular effect on them of a particular quality of a supervisor in relation to a particular case" (2002a, p. 958). The relevant parameters of fit comprised personality characteristics, interpersonal style, and theory. The specificity of fit was clearly identifiable in many instances, e.g., "One candidate found that a characterological quality of calm steadiness in her supervisor quieted and balanced her experience of being overstimulated by an exhibitionistic patient" (2002a, p. 951). The candidate selected this supervisor to supervise the case before she chose to work with this particular patient. In a supervision course Kantrowitz gave recently, the *match* among supervisee/patient/supervisor seemed "the most important variable" (Kantrowitz, personal communication). Yet Kantrowitz

> [has also emphasized] that the nature and helpfulness of the match cannot be predicted in advance, for several reasons. One is that what is manifest in each of the participants does not reveal all that potentially may emerge; different people bring out different aspects of each other. Another reason is that interactions among the three participants and their specific characteristics evolve and change over the course of the work (p. 964) . . . The dynamic interplay of patient and candidate may yield surprises. Patients may evoke conflicts in candidates that were insufficiently analyzed, or that did not emerge in their analyses. (p. 960)

The Budapest Institute's approach to supervision intrinsically addressed these issues; yet, as the following example demonstrates, such work can be done in "non-Hungarian" supervision, if the fit is right. In the following example, the *supervisor's* listening to *himself* after responding in a particular way to his supervisee, and sharing this with her began a process with this supervisee that led to a significant educational experience—for both of them.

Illustration 2

Dr. P is an advanced analytic candidate at the Institute of Contemporary Psychoanalysis in Los Angeles, whose third control case I was supervising. Dr. P was in analysis with a colleague, and conveyed how important that work continued to be for her. Yet she valued the opportunity to present her analytic work with the "free-associative" openness of sharing that characterizes the Hungarian psychoanalytic approach.

I would emphasize that, in my experience as a supervisor, the way Dr. P and I worked together does not ubiquitously happen, even with candidates at this Institute. While the purposes of supervisory work are always clear—discovering and facilitating how that supervisee and her particular patient, and how she and I, may work best together—how we advance these objectives varies widely. Methods of working range from the formal presentation by the student of her account of the analytic hour as she has recorded it (in various ways and at various times), to a way that an observer would find similar in tone and ambience, and to some extent in content, to an analytic session.

Specificities of the latter method emerged as salient in substantial measure for Dr. P and myself in our process. A specific aspect of fit between Dr P and myself that contributed to the productive operation of our particular supervisory process was our ability to co-create an ambience in which we could comfortably discuss personal aspects of who we are that emerged in process that might be affecting our supervisory work, and their possible effect on the therapeutic process of Dr. P with her patient. This does not necessarily mean that this way of working is "better" than others. It does mean that this is the way Dr. P and I worked best together.

As Dr. P. was about to leave after a supervisory session, I found myself telling her about my work with a patient that reflected problems similar to those with which she was struggling with her patient, N. I was at the time aware of a certain internal pressure to share my experience with her.

After Dr. P. left, I reflected on what I had done, and as we began our next supervision session, I shared my thoughts with Dr. P—that it seemed to be a curious kind of "narcissistic" behavior. I had felt a need to have her hear what *I* had to say, since she had done virtually all the talking in that session. I added that I was also wondering whether this was what Dr. P needed to do in that session.

I told her that in my view, she was doing excellent analytic work as she struggled with the problems presented by her patient, and that what she may have indeed needed from me during the last supervision session was in fact to listen to her, and to experience my quiet validation. I wondered, too, whether my reaction could also be understood as expressing a measure of competitiveness with Dr. P, a competitiveness that may have been stirred up not only by my need to be heard, but also by my unconsciously resonating, as it were, with competitiveness between Dr. P and her patient, an acupuncturist who had been seeing a patient of her own "like an analyst," as Dr. P had put it, several times a week.

Dr. P expressed gratitude for my candor about both of us. She had been puzzled about my extending the session; she was aware that I probably needed to stop (a light indicated the presence of someone in the waiting room) yet I did not, and was telling her about my patient. In our further discussion, she told me that she really likes when I my share anything with her—whether it be case material, theory, personal experience, or my recent trip to Greece (a country that has particular family significance for her), etc.—especially when she sees that I am enthusiastic and animated about it. She conveyed that she finds this most engaging. "So I guess I sort of enjoyed getting the extra time that day, even though I felt slightly guilty knowing your patient was waiting!" She added that all these feelings likely tied in with the complexity of her pleasure-cum-guilt about being a favored sibling. And she did think it likely that these feelings reflected issues with which she and her patient were struggling, about which she would like to learn more. She also felt there were other aspects of our process that were relevant to her work with this patient.

Dr. P was aware that she "had done all the talking" in the last supervision session—in effect, she had alluded to it with a tad of guilt during the session itself—yet she was also aware that since she hadn't seen me for several weeks, there was a whole lot to tell me in a short time, in order to catch me up. She allowed that she did tend to talk a good deal in her supervisions, as this helped her to clarify for herself what was happening in the analytic work with her patient. In other words, this was a cardinal way in which Dr P learned. She was also aware that she could be "dominant"; and, as a result of discussing our experiences and thoughts about this, she had begun to consider that in taking up so much of the talking time in her supervisions, she might, at times, have been interfering with her learning experience. She told me, "You did indeed pick up on something I have been unaware of. That [part of] it has been a blind spot . . ." Dr. P conveyed that she did find value in my ideas and perspectives—which was evident to me in many discussions we had had—yet at this time, with this patient, she was especially grateful for her experience of me as an attentive and perceptive listener. With regard to my acknowledged "countertransference" reaction, which I would more accurately term a "specific relational disruption" (see p. 104, this book), she wondered whether her tendency to be "dominating" in her interactions might have triggered an experience in me that reflected problems with which I had struggled with my mother, which she had read about in a published paper (Bacal, 2006). I told Dr. P that my mother did listen to me, but that her reaction of "superior knowingness" that I had written about was not how I experienced Dr. P. Rather, I thought my reaction to Dr. P's monopolizing the talking time in that session likely reflected a residue of my feeling eclipsed, long ago, by the liveliness of a similarly bright younger sister.

Interestingly, in our supervisory process, disruptively matching specificities[14] of connection were emerging across our dyads: Dr. P with her patient and me with Dr. P. Dr. P responded by telling me that in her interaction with important others, including her analyst, she greatly valued knowing about the other person.

As we were talking in this way, Dr P told me that she was now thinking about further experience with her patient, N. She did recall that N was indeed doing a kind of "analysis" with one of her acupuncture patients, but had not been consciously aware that this may have evoked some competitiveness within her in relation to N. She had felt more like N was doing this as a way to feel close to her, even merge with her. Yet, Dr P recognized that this also appeared to be suffused with conflict.

While N had felt seduced by her mother's attention, she struggled to free herself from her mother's need for her to serve as an accommodating archaic selfobject. I commented that N had apparently been making progress in respect of this conflict. During a recent European vacation with her parents, on which N's sister was not invited, she had been able to leave for a week and enjoy a holiday bicycling in Rome, on her own, about which Dr. P jokingly remarked to me that this was more than she would attempt! Dr. P was initially surprised, though, when N "cut me out completely" when N returned from her vacation. Dr. P sensed that N might be suffering from a guilt-laden depressiveness that was also likely overdetermined. She understood this as N's guilt about feeling that Dr. P was more important to her than her mother. Dr. P also interpreted that N may have been enjoying her time away not just from her parents, but from *her*, too, while she was bicycling and tango dancing her way through Rome. She understood this as N's "not wanting to have to worry about my missing her and having difficulty with the separation, like her mother does." N quite agreed with these interpretations.

I shared with Dr. P my recollection of how her awareness of struggling with her own guilt (which she had spontaneously shared with me earlier on) about her experience of being preferred by her parents in certain ways over her own sister, has also been helpful to Dr. P in resonating with analogous issues in the relationship with this patient. I further shared with Dr. P that I had also wondered whether my "enactment" at the end of our supervision session last week was derived in part from some mutually dissociated awareness (see Donnel Stern, 2004) from feelings variously operating within Dr P and myself about being cut out and cutting out with regard to more than one sister-related dyad. Dr. P's response was that our discussion about this felt "very useful and apt";

and that the themes of competitiveness (both "sibling" and "oedipal") that were highlighted by my sharing of my "reaction" (to her earlier monopolization of the talking time) were valuable and useful, "since I may tend to deny and minimize due to guilt about various triumphs in my family (my mother/sister/siblings). It's also really interesting to hear about your mother/sister stuff and how that may have interfaced with my stuff in the process."

Our discussion of these experiences were illuminating and valuable for me as well as for Dr. P. Its usefulness for the treatment of Dr. P's patient became especially apparent when Dr. P and I looked closely at the particularities of our own process. I also learned more about how Dr. P learned, and how—and why—I, and Dr. P, might at times find ourselves interfering with her learning.

My account of this work with Dr. P illustrates how supervision informed by specificity theory may not only enhance its effect, but also illuminate aspects of the supervisory process. We can see, in the interactions between Dr. P and myself in these supervisory sessions, as well as to some extent between Dr. L and Dr. James described by Ekstein and Wallerstein, how considering the specificity of process offers opportunities for the enhancement of learning in two major ways: through focusing attention on the particularities of that supervisor-supervisee process, along with those of that analyst-analyand dyad and on how these systems reciprocally affect one another.

The focus on the specificity of process with Dr. P also illuminates how understanding of what is traditionally regarded as separate occurrences of transference and countertransference or aspects of a mysterious "parallel process" can be enhanced by apprehending them as reflections of the specificity of interfacing processes.

The value of maintaining both personal therapy and supervised work as pillars for the training of psychoanalytic therapists continues to be widely recognized. Yet, the nature of the variegated, and particular, learning needs of each student in treating that patient optimally may emerge in either setting; and the extent to which they may—or may not—be effectively responded to, in either setting, will be discovered within the specificity of the unfolding process of its particular participants.

CONCLUSION

Therapeutic and pedagogic effect are specific to the process of the particular dyad. Psychotherapeutic process, and the process of teaching and learning it comprise the operation, and inter-relation, of unique systems that offer unique opportunities within which to respond optimally. In concluding, though, I will be faithful to this theory by re-stating it as the "specificity" of *my* experience as analyst and analysand, and as supervisee and supervisor, and invite you to consider its usefulness within your own analogous experience. Mine has taught me that when a supervisee and supervisor or patient and therapist meet, they potentially bring to their process everything about who they are at the time that may be evoked in context, and that the recognition of this, and how it unfolds and changes, will be critical in both situations. Specificity theory recognizes that the specificity of process that this entails may include but also will transcend the application of any formal theory or technique, with regard to either "treatment" or "training." Both participants must continuously find out how they need to be and what they need to do and continuously learn how they can be, and what they can do, together. Both therapeutic and pedagogic potential will be determined by how each participant *specifically* affects the other and how each can respond to the other in their process.

We believe that the perspectives of specificity theory implicitly underlie the way good therapists and good supervisors have always worked. Perhaps our central contribution has been to emphasize this by conceptualizing the power of specificity in psychotherapy and in the education for practicing it as best we can.

NOTES

1. Supervision, personal analysis, and lectures on theory comprise the three pillars of training to become a psychoanalyst.

2. Interestingly, we see here, as early as 1936, that analysts were using the term "counter-transference" to refer to all the feelings that the analyst may have toward the patient."

3. See Fleming and Benedek (1966, pp. 13–15) for a further account of what transpired at some of these conferences with regard to psychoanalytic training.

4. Fleming and Benedek (1966, p. 14) clarify that the word "control" has a stricter and more limiting connotation in English than in German. In German, the word "Kontrolle" translates as "*supervision* in the first place and *checking in the second.*"

5. Fleming and Benedek remind us that Freud, in 1910, "recognized that an analyst can learn only as far as his complexes permit"(Fleming & Benedek, 1966, p. 30).

6. Marshall (1993) provides a humorous, but trenchant, account of the development of psychoanalytic supervision over the years in a mock interview with Ernest Jones.

7. Balint had already conducted such groups for general physicians in Hungary; but this work had become constrained by the presence of other, pro-Nazi government, "supervisors." See Haynal (1989, pp. 109–110).

8. Balint, in his own groups, distinguished between the "public" and the "private" transference of the doctor (1957, p. 312).

9. Two notable exceptions have been in the books on supervision by Ekstein and Wallerstein 1958) and Fleming and Benedek (1966).

10. According to Andre Haynal (personal communication, 2010), this tradition has been lost over the years, although attempts are being made, by himself and others, "to come back to the heritage of Ferenczi and his colleagues."

11. Ekstein and Wallerstein do not tell us anything about the particular supervisor, and how he may have contributed to the particularity of the process.

12. In advocating that the candidate's first case should be supervised during his personal analysis, the Hungarian analysts regarded their task as addressing his unresolved personal problems that precluded effective work with his analytic "control" case, i.e., "Kontrollanalyse" (see pp. 129–30 this chapter).

13. In a supervision course Kantrowitz gave recently, what emerged as "the most important variable" . . . was the *match* among supervisee/patient/supervisor (Kantrowitz, personal communication). What also follows from Kantrowitz's studies is the recognition that "selection" for supervisor and for supervisee is optimally mutual. When a "Mutual Selection Interview" was instituted at the Tavistock Clinic with regard to participation by physicians in groups for training in the psychological aspects of their work ("Balint Groups"), the success of the program appeared to increase (Balint, M., Balint, E., Gosling, R., & Hildebrand, P., 1966).

14. Sander (2002, p. 19) refers to Weiss's (1970) assertion "that the determining quality of specificity is a principle, universally used in the living world . . . [that] is essential for communication, recognition, affinity relations, selectivity, and so on. Weiss (1970) described the basic principle as one of matched specificities—'a sort of resonance between two systems attuned to each other by corresponding properties'".

References

Alexander, F. (1956). *Psychoanalysis and Psychotherapy: Developments in Theory, Technique and Training.* New York: Norton.

Aristotle. *Nicomachean Ethics.*

Aron, L. (1996). *A Meeting of Minds.* Hillsdale, NJ: Analytic Press.

———. (2006). Analytic impasse and the third: Clinical implications of intersubjectivity theory. *Int. J. Psycho-Anal.,* 87:349–368.

———. (2006). *IARPP Online Colloquium.* October 3–November 19, 2006.

Aronson, S. (2000). Analytic supervision: All work and no play? *Contemp. Psychoanal.,* 36:121–132.

Axline, V. (1964). *Dibs in Search of Self.* New York: Ballantine.

Bacal, H. (1971). Training in psychological medicine: An attempt to assess Tavistock Clinic seminars. *Psychiatry in Medicine,* Vol. 2, 13–22.

———. (1972). Balint groups: Training or treatment? *Psychiatry in Medicine,* Vol. 3, 373–377.

———. (1975a). The treatment aspect of Balint training. *Journal of the Balint Society,* 4:10–13.

———. (1975b). The doctor as a prescription for his patient. *Canadian Family Physician,* 103–110.

———. (1985). Optimal responsiveness and the therapeutic process. In *Optimal Responsiveness: How Therapists Heal Their Patients,* ed. H. Bacal. Northvale, NJ: Jason Aronson, 3–34.

———. (1987). British object-relations theorists and self psychology: Some critical reflections. *Internat. J. Psycho-Anal.,* 68:81–98.

———. (1990). The elements of a corrective selfobject experience. *Psychoanal. Inq.,* 10:347–372.

———. (1994). The selfobject relationship in psychoanalytic treatment. In *A Decade of Progress: Progress in Self Psychology,* Vol. 10, ed. A. Goldberg. Hillsdale, NJ: The Analytic Press, 21–30.

——. (1998). *Optimal Responsiveness: How Therapists Heal Their Patients.* Northvale, NJ: Jason Aronson.

——. (2006). Specificity theory: Conceptualizing a personal and professional quest for therapeutic possibility. *Internat. J. Psychoanal. Self Psychol.*, 1:133–155.

Bacal, H. & Carlton, L. (2008). Specificity theory: Discovering therapeutic efficacy in the specificity of process, *paper presented at the winter meetings of the American Psychoanalytic Association, New York,* January 20, 2008.

——. (2010a). Who can do what, therapeutically, with whom, in what way? *J. Psychother. Integration,* Vol. 20, No. 1, 46–50.

——. (2010b). Kohut's last words on analytic cure and how we hear them now—A view from specificity theory. *Int. J. Psychoanal. Self Psychology,* 5: 132–143.

Bacal, H. and Herzog, B. (2003). Specificity theory and optimal responsiveness: An outline. *Psychoanalytic Psychology,* Vol. 20, No. 4, 635–648.

Bacal, H. and Newman, K. (1990). *Theories of Object relations: Bridges to Self Psychology.* New York: Columbia University Press.

Bacal, H. and Thomson, P. (1996). The psychoanalyst's selfobject needs and the effect of their frustration on the treatment: A new view of countertransference. In *Basic Ideas Reconsidered: Progress in Self Psychology,* ed. A. Goldberg. Hillsdale, NJ: The Analytic Press, 17–35.

——. (1998). Optimal responsiveness and the therapist's reaction to the patient's unresponsiveness. In *Optimal Responsiveness: How Therapists Heal their Patients,* ed. H. Bacal. Northvale, NJ: Jason Aronson, 249–270.

Balint, A. (1935). Communication reported by Glover, E., 1935, Four Countries Conference. *Bul. Int. Psychoanalytic Assoc.,* 16:505–509.

Balint, E. (1967). Training as an impetus to ego-development. *The Psychoanalytic Forum,* Vol. 2, No. 1, 55–62.

Balint, E., Courtenay, M., Elder, A., Hull, S., & Julian, P. (1993). *The Doctor, the Patient, and the Group.* London: Routledge.

Balint, M. (1937). Early developmental states of the ego: Primary object-love. In *Primary Love and Psycho-Analytic Technique,* 74–90.

——. (1948). On the psycho-analytic training system. *Int. J. Psycho-Anal.,* 29:163–173.

——. (1957). *The Doctor, His Patient, and the Illness.* London: Pitman Medical.

——. (1968). *The Basic Fault.* London: Tavistock.

——. (1969). The structure of the training-cum-research seminars. *J. Roy. Coll. Gen. Practit,* 17:201–211.

Balint, M. & Balint, A. (1939). On transference and counter-transference. *Int. J. Psycho-Anal.,* 20:223–230.

Balint, M. & Balint, E. (1961). *Psychotherapeutic Techniques in Medicine.* London: Tavistock.

Balint, M. , Balint, E., Gosling, R., & Hildebrand, P. (1966). *A Study of Doctors.* London: Tavistock.

Baudry, F. (1993). The personal dimension and management of the supervisory situation with special note on the parallel process. *Psychoanal. Q.,* 62:588–614.

Bedau, M. & Humphreys, P. (2008). Eds. *Emergence: Contemporary Readings in Philosophy and Science.* Cambridge, MA: The MIT Press.

Beebe, B. and F. Lachmann (2002). *Infant Research and Adult Treatment: Co-Constructing Interactions.* Hillsdale, NJ: The Analytic Press.

Benjamin, J. (2004). Beyond doer and done to: An intersubjective view of thirdness. *Psychoanalytic Q.* Vol. LXXIII, No. 1, 5–46.

Bion, W. R. (1967). Notes on memory and desire. *Psychoanalytic Forum,* Vol 3, 271–280.

Bird, B. (1972). Notes on transference: Universal phenomenon and hardest part of analysis. *J. Amer. Psychoanal. Assn.,* 20:267–301.

Blum, H. (1986). Countertransference and the theory of technique: Discussion. *J. Amer. Psychoanal. Assn.,* 34:309–328.

Brandchaft, B. (2004). To free the spirit from its cell. In *The Intersubjective Perspective,* ed. R. Stolorow, G. Atwood, and B. Brandchaft. Northvale, NJ: Jason Aronson, 57–76.

———. (2007). Systems of pathological accommodation and change in analysis. *Psychoanal. Psychol.,* 24:667–687.

Brothers, L. (2002). *Mistaken Identity: The Mind-Brain Problem Reconsidered* (SUNY Series in Science, Technology, and Society). New York: State University of New York Press.

Brower, B. (2000). Contextualism, epistemological. In *Concise Encyclopedia of Philosophy.* London: Routledge, 174.

Carlton, L. (2009). Making sense of self and systems in psychoanalysis: Summation essay for the 30th Annual International Conference on the Psychology of the Self. *Int. J. Psychoanal. Self Psychol.,* 4:313–329.

Cilliers, P. (1998). *Complexity and Postmodernism.* New York: Routledge.

Coburn, W. (2002). A world of systems: The role of systemic patterns of experience in the therapeutic process. *Psychoanalytic Inq.,* 5:655–677.

Connors, M. (2010). Symptom-focused dynamic psychotherapy. *J. of Psychother. Integration.,* Vol. 20, No. 1, 37–45.

Dewald, P. (1981) Aspects of the supervisory process. *Ann. Psychoanal.,* 9:75–89.

Doehrman, M. (1976). Parallel processes in supervision and psychotherapy. *Bulletin of the Meninger Clinic,* 40, 3–104.

Edelman, G. (1987). *Neural Darwinism: The Theory of Neuronal Group Selection.* New York: Basic Books.

———. (1988). *Topobiology: An Introduction to Molecular Embryology.* New York: Basic Books.

———. (1989). *The Remembered Present: A Biological Theory of Consciousness.* New York: Basic Books.

———. (1992). *Bright Air, Brilliant Fire.* New York: Basic Books.

———. (1998). Building a picture of the brain. *Daedulus,* Vol. 127 (2): 37–69.

———. (2004). *Wider Than the Sky.* New Haven: Yale University Press.

Edelman, G. and Tononi, G. (1995) Neural darwinism: the brain as a selectional system. In *Nature's Imagination: The Frontiers of Scientific Vision,* ed. John Cornwell. Oxford University Press, 78–121.

Eissler, K. (1953). The effect of the structure of the ego on psychoanalytic technique. *J. Amer. Psychoanal. Assn.,* 1:104–143.

Ekstein, R. & Wallerstein, R. (1958). *The Teaching and Learning of Psychotherapy.* New York: International Universities Press.

Eyesenck, H. (1952). The effects of psychotherapy, an evaluation. *J. Cons. Psychol.*, 16:319.

Ferenczi, S. (1909). Letter from Sándor Ferenczi to Sigmund Freud, August 11, 1909.

——. (1928). The elasticity of psychoanalytic technique. In *Final Contributions to the Problems and Methods of Psychoanalysis*. London: Hogarth, 87–101.

Fiscalini, J. (1994). The uniquely interpersonal and the interpersonally unique—On interpersonal psychoanalysis. *Contemp. Psychoanal.*, 30:114–134.

Fleming, J. & Benedek, T. (1966). *Psychoanalytic Supervision*. New York: Grune & Stratton.

Foehl, J. (2010). The play's the thing: The primacy of process and the persistence of pluralism in Contemporary Psychoanalysis. *Contemp. Psychoanal.*, 46:48–86.

Fosshage, J. (1994). Toward reconceptualizing transference: Theoretical and clinical considerations. *Int. J. Psycho-Anal.*, 75, 265–280.

——. (1995). Countertransference as the analyst's experience of the analysand: Influence of listening perspectives. *Psychoanalytic Psychology*, 12(3):375–391.

——. (1998). Optimal responsiveness and listening/experiencing perspectives. In *Optimal Responsiveness: How Therapists Heal Their Patients*, ed. H. Bacal. Northvale, NJ: Jason Aronson, 1998, 117–139.

Freud, S. (1900). *The Interpretation of Dreams. S.E. IV-V*

——. (1912a). The dynamics of transference. *S.E. XII.*

——. (1912b). Recommendations to physicians practising psycho-analysis. *S.E. XII.*

——. (1915). Observations on transference-love (Further Recommendations on the Technique of Psycho-Analysis III). *S.E. XII.*

——. (1919). Lines of advance in psycho-analytic therapy. *S.E. XVII.*

Gadamer, H-G. (1975). *Truth and Method, second revised edition*. New York: Continuum.

——. (1979). The problem of historical consciousness. In *Interpretive Social Science: A Reader* ed. P. Rabinow and W. Sullivan, 103–160.

Galatzer-Levy, R. (2002). Emergence. *Psychoanalytic Inq.* 5:708–739.

——. (2007). *Presentation to International Association of Psychoanalytic Self Psychology Annual Conference, Los Angeles,* October 11, 2007.

Gediman, H. & Wolkenfeld, F. (1980). The parallelism phenomenon in psychoanalysis and supervision: Its reconsideration as a triadic system. *Psychoanal. Q.*, 49:234–255.

Gladwell, M. (1995). *Blink*. New York: Little, Brown and Company.

Gosling, R., Miller, D., Turquet, P., & Woodhouse, D. (1967). *The Use of Small Groups in Training*. Grune & Stratton.

Grey, A., & Fiscalini, J. (1987). Parallel process as transference-countertransference interaction. *Psychoanal. Psychol.*, 4:131–144.

Guntrip, H. (1975). My experience of analysis with Fairbairn and Winnicott. *Internat. Rev. Psychoanal.*, 2:145–156.

Haynal, A. (1989). *Controversies in Psychoanalytic Method: From Freud and Ferenczi to Michael Balint*. New York: New York University Press.

Heimann, P. (1950). On counter-transference. *Int. J. Psycho-Anal.*, 31:81–84.

Herzog, B. (1998). Optimal responsiveness and the experience of sharing. In *Optimal Responsiveness: How Therapists Heal Their Patients*, ed. H. Bacal. Northvale, NJ: Jason Aronson, 175–190.

Hoffman, I. (1983). The patient as interpreter of the analyst's experience. *Contemp. Psychoanal.*, 19:389–422.

IARPP online colloquium, October 30–November 19, 2006.

Isakower, O. (1963). Problems of supervision (*Faculty of New York Psychoanal. Inst.*).

Kantrowitz, J. (2002a). The Triadic match: The interactive effect of supervisor, candidate, and patient. *J. Amer. Psychoanal. Assn.*, 50:939–96.

———. (2002b). The external observer and the lens of the patient-analyst match. *Int. J. Psycho-Anal.* 83:339–350.

Keiser, S. (1969). Psychoanalysis—Taught, Learned, and Experienced. *J. Amer. Psychoanal. Assn.*, 17:238–267.

Kindler, A. (1998). Optimal responsiveness and psychoanalytic supervision. In *Optimal Responsiveness: How Therapists Heal Their Patients*, ed. H. Bacal. Northvale, NJ: Jason Aronson, 357–382.

———. (2010). Spontaneity and improvisation in psychoanalysis. *Psychoanal. Inq.* Vol. 30:3, 222–235.

Kim, J. (2008). Making sense of emergence. In *Emergence: Contemporary Readings in Philosophy and Science*, ed. M. Bedau & P. Humphreys. Cambridge, MA: The MIT Press, 127–153.

Kohut, H. (1971). *The Analysis of the Self*. New York: International Universities Press.

———. (1977). *The Restoration of the Self*. New York: International Universities Press.

———. (1981). On empathy. In: *The Search for the Self. Selected Writings of Heinz Kohut 1950–1978*, ed. P. Ornstein. Madison, CT: International Universities Press, 529.

———. (1984). *How Does Analysis Cure?* A. Goldberg and P. Stepansky, eds. Chicago: University of Chicago Press.

Kohut, H. and Wolf, E. (1978). The disorders of the self and their treatment: An outline. *Int. J. Psychoanal.* 59:413–425.

Kovacs, V. (1936), Training-and control-analysis. *Int. J. Psycho-Anal.*, 17:346–354.

Lachmann, F. (1986). Interpretation of Psychic Conflict and Adversarial Relationships: A Self-Psychological Perspective. *Psychoanal. Psychol.* 3(4):341–55.

———. (2008). *Transforming Narcissism: Reflections on Empathy, Humor, and Expectations*. New York: The Analytic Press.

———. (2010). Going home. *Int. J. Psychoanalytic Self Psychology*, Vol. 5, No. 2, 144–159.

Lawrence, D. H. (1936). *Phoenix: The Posthumous Papers*, Vol. I, ed. E. McDonald. New York: Penguin Books, 1980, 377–378.

Lesser, R. (1983). Supervision: Illusions, anxieties and questions. *Contemp. Psychoanal.*, 19: 120–129.

Levine, M. (1972). *Psychiatry and Ethics*. New York: G. Braziller.

Levy, J. and Parnell, Y. (2001). The benefits and hazards of working through the supervisee's countertransference in psychoanalytic supervision. *J. of Clinical Psychoanalysis*, Vol. 10, No. 1, 91–116.

Lewis, J. (2009). *IAPSP website communication*, Nov. 14, 2009.

Lichtenberg (2005). *Craft and Spirit*. Hillsdale, NJ: The Analytic Press.

Lyons-Ruth, K. (2000). "I sense that you sense that I Sense . . .": Sander's recognition process and the specificity of relational moves in the psychotherapeutic setting. *Infant Mental Health Journal*, Vol. 21 (1–2):85–98.

——. (2006). The interface between attachment and intersubjectivity: Perspective from the longitudinal study of disorganized attachment. *Psychoanal. Inq.*, 26:595–616.

Malan, D., Bacal, H., Heath, S., and Balfour, F. (1968). A study of psychodynamic changes in untreated neurotic patients—I. *The British Journal of Psychiatry*, Vol. 114, No. 510, 525–551.

Malan, D., Heath, S., Bacal, H., Balfour, H. (1975). Psychodynamic changes in untreated neurotic patients—II. Apparently Genuine Improvements. *Archives of General Psychiatry*, January, Vol. 32.

Malan, D. and Della Selva, P. (2006). *Lives Transformed*. London: Karnac.

Maroda, K. (2010). Self-Disclosure and advice: Understanding how and when the therapist's disclosures are therapeutic. In *Psychodynamic Techniques: Working with Emotion in the Therapeutic Relationship*, ed. K. Maroda. Guilford, 107–135.

Marshall, R. (1993). Perspectives on supervision: Tea and/or supervision. *Mod. Psychoanal.* 18:45–57.

Miletic, M. J. (1998). Prologue. *Psychoanal. Inq.*, 18:515–517.

Miller, L. and Twomey, J. (1999). A parallel without a process: A relational view of a supervisory experience. *Contemp. Psychoanal.*, 35:557–580.

Mitchell, S. (1997). *Influence and Autonomy in Psychoanalysis*. Hillsdale NJ: Analytic Press.

Moore, B. and Fine, B. (1995). *Psychoanalytic Terms and Concepts*. Yale: New Haven.

Nahum, J. (2005). The "Something More" than interpretation revisited: Sloppiness and co-creativity in the psychoanalytic encounter. *J. Amer. Psychoanal. Assn.*, 53:693–729.

Natterson, J. (1991). *Beyond Countertransference*. Northvale, NJ: Jason Aronson.

Orange, D., and Stolorow, R. (1998). Self-disclosure from the perspective of intersubjectivity theory. *Psychoanal. Inq.*, 18:530–537.

Pally, R. (1998). Emotional processing: The mind-body connection. *Int. J. Psycho-Anal.*, 79:349–362.

Parsons, M. (1999). The logic of play in psychoanalysis. *Int. J. Psycho-Anal.*, 80:871–884.

Pizer, S. (1998). *Building Bridges: Negotiation of Paradox in Psychoanalysis*. Hillsdale, NJ: Analytic Press.

Prigogine, I. (1996). *The End of Certainty*. New York: Free Press. Psychoanalytic Inquiry, 2010 Vol. 30:3.

Pulver, S. (1984). Psychoanalytic Supervision: A Method of Clinical Teaching: By Joan Fleming and Therese F. Benedek. Republished In Classics in Psychoanalysis, Monograph No. 1. New York: International Universities Press 1983. *Int. J. Psycho-Anal.*, 65:489–492.

Racker, H. (1968). *Transference and Countertransference*. London: Karnac.

Renik, O. (1995). The ideal of the anonymous analyst and the problem of self-disclosure. *Psychoanal. Q.*, 64:466–495.

Ricci, W. and Broucek, F. (1998). Optimal responsiveness and neutrality, abstinence, and anonymity. In *Optimal Responsiveness: How Therapists Heal Their Patients*, ed. H. Bacal. Northvale, NJ: Jason Aronson, 35–57.

Richetta, M. (2010). Knowing Eleanor: Her life from the perspectives of complexity theory and specificity theory (*submitted in partial fulfillment of the requirements for the degree of Psy.D., Institute of Contemporary Psychoanalysis,* Los Angeles).

Ringstrom, P. (2001). Cultivating the improvisational in psychoanalytic treatment. *Psychoanal. Dial.*, 11:727–754.

——. (2010). Principles of improvisation: A model of therapeutic play in relational psychoanalysis. (*Unpublished*).

Rosbrow, T. (1997). From parallel process to developmental process: A developmental plan/formulation approach to supervision. In *Conversations in Self Psychology. Progress in Self Psychology,* Vol. 13, ed. A. Goldberg. Hillsdale, NJ: The Analytic Press, 149–164.

Rosenblum, S. (1998). Absence anonymity and the avoidance of self-disclosure. *Psychoanal. Inq.*, 118:538–549.

Rycroft, C. (1968). *A Critical Dictionary of Psychoanalysis.* Harmondsworth, Middlesex: Penguin Books.

Sacks, O. (1995). A new vision of the mind. In *Nature's Imagination: The Frontiers of Scientific Vision,* ed. J. Cornwell. Oxford University Press, 101–12.

Sander, L.W. (1995). Identity and the experience of specificity in a process of recognition: Commentary on Seligman and Shanok. *Psychoanal. Dial.*, 5:579–593.

——. (2002). Thinking differently: Principles of process in living systems and the specificity of being known. *Psychoanal. Dial.*, 12(1):11–42.

Sandler, J. (1976). Countertransference and role-responsiveness. *Int. R. Psychoanal.*, 3:43–47.

Schore, A. (2003). *Affect Regulation and the Repair of the Self.* New York: WW Norton & Co.

Schwaber, E. (1981). Empathy: A mode of analytic listening. *Psychoanal. Inq.*, 1:357–391.

——. (2010). Reflections on Heinz Kohut's last presentation, "On Empathy," 1981: Its impact on my own pathway. *Int. J. Psychoanal. Self Psychology,* 5: 160–176.

Searles, H. (1955). The informational value of the supervisor's emotional experiences. *Psychiatry*, 18:135–146.

Segal, H. (1973). *Introduction to the Work of Melanie Klein. New, enlarged edition.* London: The Hogarth Press.

Shane, M. and Shane, E. (1995). Un-American activities and other dilemmas experienced in the supervision of candidates. *Psychoanal. Inq.*, 15:226–239.

Siegel, D. (1999). *The Developing Mind: How Relationships and the Brain Interact to Shape How We Are.* New York: The Guildford Press.

Solnit, A. (1970). Learning from psychoanalytic supervision. *Int. J. Psycho-Anal.*, 51:359–362.

Sperry, M. (2007). Discussion of Linda Marino's paper, "Who is analysis for? The candidate's dilemma." *Paper presented at the 30th Annual International Conference on the Psychology of the Self, Los Angeles,* October 12, 2007.

Spruiell, V. (1993). Deterministic chaos and the sciences of complexity: Psychoanalysis in the midst of a general scientific revolution. *J. Amer. Psychoanal. Assn.* 41: 3–44.

Stern, D., Sander, L, Nahum, J., Harrison, A., Lyons-Ruth, K. Morgan, A. Bruschweilerstern, and Tronick, E. (1998). Non-interpretive mechanisms in psychoanalytic therapy: The 'Something More' than interpretation. *Int. J. psycho-Anal.* 79:903–921.

Stern, Donnel, (2004). The Eye Sees Itself: Dissociation, Enactment, and the Achievement of Conflict. Contemp. *Psychoanal.*, 40:197–237.

Stolorow, R. (1994). Converting psychotherapy to psychoanalysis. In *The Intersubjective Perspective,* ed. R. Stolorow, G. Atwood & B. Brandchaft. Northvale, NJ: Jason Aronson.

——. (2006). Intersubjective systems theory. In *The Edinburgh International Encyclopaedia of Psychoanalysis,* ed. R. Skelton. Edinburgh: Edinburgh University Press, 250.

Stolorow, R. and Atwood, G. (1979). *Faces in a Cloud.* Northvale, NJ: Jason Aronson.

——. (1992). *Contexts of Being: The Intersubjective Foundations of Psychological Life.* Hillsdale, NJ: The Analytic Press.

——. (1997). Deconstructing the myth of the neutral analyst: An alternative from intersubjective systems theory. *Psychoanalytic Quarterly,* 66: 431–449.

Stolorow, R., Brandchaft, B., & Atwood, G. (1987). *Psychoanalytic Treatment, An Intersubjective Approach.* Hillsdale, NJ: Analytic Press.

Stolorow. R. & Orange, D. (1998). Self-disclosure from the perspective of intersubjectivity theory. *Psychoanal. Inq.* 18:530–537.

Terman, D. (1998). Optimal responsiveness and a new view of structuralization. In *Optimal Responsiveness: How Therapists Heal Their Patients,* ed. H. Bacal. Northvale, NJ: Jason Aronson, 59–74.

Thelen, E. (2005) Dynamic systems theory and the complexity of change. *Psychoanal. Dial.,* 15:255–283.

Thelen, E., & Smith, L. B. (1994). *A Dynamic Systems Approach to the Development of Perception and Action.* Cambridge, MA: MIT Press.

Tolpin, M. (2002). Doing psychoanalysis of normal development: Forward edge transferences. In *Progress in Self Psychology: Postmodern Self Psychology,* Vol. 18, ed. A. Goldberg. Hillsdale, NJ: Analytic Press, 167–190.

Tronick, E. (1998). Dyadically expanded states of consciousness and the process of therapeutic change. *Infant Mental Health Journal,* Vol. 19(3), 290–299.

——. (2003). Of course all relationships are unique: How co-creative processes generate unique mother-infant and patient-therapist relationships and change other relationships. *Psychoanal. Inq.,* 23:473–491.

——. (2005). Why is connection with others so critical? The formation of dyadic states of consciousness and the expansion of individuals' states of consciousness: Coherence governed selection and the co-creation of meaning out of messy meaning making. In *Emotional Development,* ed. J. Nadel and D. Muir. Oxford University Press, 293–315.

Trop, G., Burke, M., & Trop, J. (2002). Thinking dynamically in psychoanalytic theory and practice: A review of intersubjectivity theory. In *Postmodern Self Psy-*

chology: Progress in Self Psychology, Vol. 18, ed. A. Goldberg. Hillsdale, NJ: The Analytic Press, 129–147.

Wachtel, P. (1986) From neutrality to personal revelation: Patterns of influence in the analytic relationship (A Symposium)—On the limits of therapeutic neutrality. *Contemp. Psychoanal.* 22:60–70.

Weinshel, E. (1988). Play and playing in adults and in adult psychoanalysis: An addendum to the paper "On Inconsolability." *Bul. Anna Freud Centre,* 11:108–127.

Weisel-Barth, J. (2006). Thinking and writing about complexity theory, *Int. J. Psychoanal. Self Psychol.*, Vol. 1, No. 4, pp. 365–388.

Winnicott, D. (1971a). *Playing and Reality*. London: Tavistock.

——. (1971b). Transitional Objects and Transitional Phenomena. In *Playing and Reality*. London: Tavistock, 1–25.

——. (1971c). *Therapeutic Consultations in Child Psychiatry*. London: The Hogarth Press.

Wolf, E. (1980). On the developmental line of selfobject relations. In *Advances in Self Psychology*, ed. A. Goldberg, New York: Int. Universities Press, 117–130.

——. 1995. How to supervise without doing harm: Comments on psychoanalytic supervision. *Psychoanal. Inq.* 15: 252–267

Index

About the Authors

Howard Bacal is a training and supervising analyst at the Institute of Contemporary Psychoanalysis and at the New Center for Psychoanalysis in Los Angeles, and supervising analyst at the Institute for the Psychoanalytic Study of Subjectivity and the National Training Program in Contemporary Psychoanalysis in New York. He has a private practice in Los Angeles.

Dr. Bacal received his medical degree at McGill University and psychiatric training at the University of Cincinnati. He qualified in adult and child psychoanalysis at the British Institute of Psychoanalysis during one of the most creatively exciting periods within the British Psychoanalytic Society, where he had the good fortune to work with some of its most brilliant thinkers, such as Michael Balint, Donald Winnicott, Marion Milner, Wilfred Bion, Charles Rycroft, and J. D. Sutherland. During this time, he studied and taught the application of psychoanalytic concepts in small groups for treatment and training at the Tavistock Clinic and Tavistock Institute of Human Relations, and collaborated with D. H. Malan in psychotherapy research. On his return to North America in the early 1970s, he studied for several years with Heinz Kohut and his colleagues at the Chicago Institute for Psychoanalysis.

Howard Bacal has written extensively on the interface between object relations theory and self psychology, and has authored many papers on the therapeutic and pedagogic process. He is recognized as a leading exponent of the relational perspective in self psychology theory, and is co-author with Kenneth Newman of *Theories of Object Relations: Bridges to Self Psychology* (Columbia University Press). His edited volume, *Optimal Responsiveness: How Therapists Heal Their Patients* (Jason Aronson), illustrates how eighteen therapists utilize the therapeutic implications of his concept of *optimal responsiveness,* the concept whose theoretical underpinning constitutes *specificity theory,* the subject of this book.

Lucyann Carlton is a training and supervising analyst at the Institute for Contemporary Psychoanalysis in Los Angeles, and she has a private practice in Irvine, California. She holds a doctorate in law and in psychoanalysis, has authored many published articles, and frequently is a presenter at psychoanalytic conferences. Lucyann is president and a member of the board of directors of the International Association for Psychoanalytic Self Psychology. She is a co-editor of neuroscience for the *International Journal of Psychoanalytic Self Psychology* and a junior editor for *Psychoanalytic Dialogues*.

Breinigsville, PA USA
17 December 2010

251608BV00004B/2/P

9 780765 707697